Your Sixth Sense

Don't be deceived

Don Gentry II

ISBN:1544868642
ISBN-13: 9781544868646

My Prayer

Holy Spirit, guide my thoughts and my words, that I might guide others to a personal relationship with you, a deeper understanding of who you are, and that they too may learn to hear your voice. I pray that the words of this book do not deviate from the Holy Word in any way, but that they help others to see how the Scriptures can come alive to each and every person who calls upon Jesus Christ, the Son of God, to be saved.

I pray for all that read the words in this book that you are able to be blessed by what the Holy Spirit says to you.

Table of Contents

My thanks

Thank you, Dad. I may have had only 14 years of life with him, but he taught me more in those 14 years than many fathers teach their children in a lifetime.

Thank you, Mom. I cannot imagine having been raised by any other. Your love and faith continue to serve as an inspiration to me. You are indeed a Proverbs 31 woman, and I, your child, rise and call you blessed. I am proud to be your son.

Thank you, my beloved wife. I would need a book to write how blessed I am to be your husband. Your undying love, your incredible support, your amazing friendship, and your love for God is a blessing beyond description. I am so blessed that God saw fit to allow me to have you as my wife and the mother of our children.

Thank you, my wonderful daughters. I am so blessed to be called your Dad. Each of you makes my heart swim with pride. Your love for God is such a wonderful gift to me. I look forward to seeing how God uses each of you as you continue to follow His will for your lives. I pray that this book helps each of you to continue to discover what His will looks like for your life.

Thank you, Tim H, to you and your family. The journey of friendship we have been on over the years has provided so much more than I can thank you for. You have encouraged and challenged me in more ways than you know.

Thank you, Terry P. You didn't know me from Adam, yet you chose to believe in me and invest in me and the ministry that God gave me. Your mentorship has inspired me, ticked me off, frustrated me, encouraged me and challenged me. I cannot say thank you enough!!

Thank you, New Hope Church, Camden, MI! You are a wonderful church. Thank you for your patience as God shaped me as a leader while I served with you! I can only hope that someday each and every one of you will know that when God called me away I had to respond in obedience.

Thank you, Matt and Journey Church, this book would not have been complete without this leg of my personal Journey! What a privilege it is to be a part of this amazing church! Blessed beyond words!

I could go on and thank many others. We are all just a composite of all the lives that have individually touched us. I am a better man because of each of you, and I thank you all.

PREFACE

I hope that this book serves as an inspiration to you as you journey toward understanding who God is in your life. I am going to share with you the information that has led me to a deep, satisfying, intimate walk with the one true God. I believe that same relationship is available to all.

Unfortunately, you and I as humans have a problem. God's church has a problem, and His Western church has an even greater problem. We neglect the power of the Holy Spirit. We misunderstand the person of the Holy Spirit. Within the church, denominations fight over who they think the Holy Spirit is and what He does. It will be my assertion that true understanding will happen when we understand the role of our Sixth Sense and the Holy Spirit.

The reason we argue over the Holy Spirit is because of doctrinal beliefs. What I am going to be proposing in this book is a theological belief system. I believe that when our theology is strong, then some of our arguments will be less divisive.

Because of our misunderstandings, our blatant hypocrisies, our genuine intentions, and our finite minds, we are all on a journey to understand the essence of the supernatural. Our Sixth Sense has been given to us that we may understand the many supernatural influences with which we must interact. The outcome of our journey is dictated by how we respond to the supernatural prompting of the Sixth Sense.

It is our ability to interact with and be guided by our Sixth Sense that separates man from animals. It is my desire that by the end of this book you can understand how to properly relate, be guided by, and keep your Sixth Sense from being deceived.

THE BEGINNING - CHPT 1

Have you ever noticed that every culture has some type of belief in God, some higher power that they serve? Have you ever wondered why that is, or who is right? For example, the Native American has The Great Spirit. The Greeks had multiple gods; many in the continent of Asia worship/honor Buddha; in the Middle East, Mohammed is a great prophet leading us on how to worship Allah, Hindus have millions of gods. I think you get the point. Why all the differences, and could one belief system be more right than another one?

Every culture, every religion, every belief about a higher power has come because of humans Sixth Sense. There is an inner voice inside in each of us that suggests that there is something bigger than ourselves “out there.” Our culture, our families, and our environment heavily influence our beliefs, but they are all start because of our sixth sense.

You were born with your five senses. I suggest that there is a still, small voice that has been written into your DNA since birth. This Sixth Sense is that sense that we all have but sometimes ignore. It is the sense that urges us on at times. It is the inner conscience that we argue with on occasion. All of us have it. All of us are aware of it. It is that sense that says there is something bigger than ourselves. It is that sense that compels us to either accept or reject religion as a valid option. It is that sense that drives us to find answers to our spiritual questions.

All our senses can be deceived. For example, I love magic tricks or illusions. I am like a little child when it comes to these shows. In my mind, I know that with a little explanation or extra observation, I can figure out how my senses are being tricked. Some performances are pretty amazing, and I find myself enjoying being deceived. I am stuck in a quandary when it comes to my love of illusions: I like to know how they work, but I like to be amazed as well.

It is the same way with all our senses. Each can be tricked, and each sense is different in all of us. Sometimes we even want them to stay tricked. If all our senses are subject to deception, then how much more can our Sixth Sense be deceived.

If our other senses are deceived, we can usually come to an understanding of what went wrong. With a little explanation, we can understand the magic trick.

It is the same way with our sixth sense. Some of us are being deceived and confused by what our sixth sense is telling us.

Just like our sense of touch protects us from touching something hot, just like our sense of sight prevents us from walking into oncoming traffic, your sixth sense, properly understood, should lead you from danger and into right living, right emotional responses, and a clear understanding of religion and truth. If all our other senses can be deceived and only corrected with proper information, instruction, medication, etc., then it stands to reason that it is the same way with our sixth sense. To properly utilize our sixth sense, we must have the proper information.

The truth is what corrects our other deceptions, and the truth is what will properly guide your sixth sense.

Our sixth sense suggests to us that there is a right way and a wrong way to live our lives. As a society, we argue about truth. Can anyone dictate or identify truth? **Our sixth sense suggests that we follow some unwritten code of conduct. Where does that unwritten code come from?**

While we may not agree on what to call this sixth sense, I know you have felt it at times. Maybe you have been fighting it. Maybe you live your life plagued by guilt, and you are tied up in knots because you can't ever seem to measure up to what your inner voice expects. Whatever your plight in life, this book has the potential to help you make sense of it all.

Let me illustrate what I mean. I am a picture kind of guy. They say a picture is worth a thousand words, so welcome to your picture book. As you will soon discover, I am not an artist; I trust that you can laugh with me as I attempt to illustrate my point. As you look at this picture and all following pictures, we are trying to get this little stick figure across the great divide. We want to get on the solid ground with our higher power. Whatever it is that our sixth sense is guiding us towards. This picture is going to represent where we are in the Journey of understanding how to respond to our sixth sense.

Our sixth sense seems to be leading us to some truth-- a higher power that we answer to as a human race. Our sixth sense suggests to us how we are supposed to live in order to please that higher power. As I said earlier every culture and civilization that we study has various ways of responding to this prompting.

There is a great ancient text talks about our inner voice in this way,

> *"They show the work of the Law written in their hearts, their conscience bearing witness and their thoughts alternately accusing or else defending them," (1)*

That text was originally written in Greek and this law that is written on their hearts is talking about our sixth sense. The original Greek word for heart here is *kardia*. You may recognize it as the word from which we derive the meaning for the organ that pumps blood through our veins. This ancient text meant something far more significant. It means the mind, character, inner self, will, intention, and center. In fact, this word is used over eight hundred times in this ancient text without ever meaning organ. (2)

This ancient text then ties *kardia* in with our conscience that accuses or defends us. In the previous text, the original Greek word for conscience is *suneidésis,* which means "persisting notion." (3) This persisting notion is designed to guide us to the higher power that is calling out to each of us. It is our responsibility to make sense of that persisting notion, and not be deceived. As you will see in the second chapter, there are many ways of thought that can deceive our sixth sense.

You may be asking yourself, "If my sixth sense can be deceived, why am I going to read this book? What if the author's sixth sense deceived him?" That is an excellent question. We should all be thinking that question when we are hearing something that could shape our minds and the way we think. We each have the responsibility to figure out the truth.

The ancient text that I quoted earlier is the Bible. As we read the scriptures, they clearly identify what or who should be guiding our sixth sense. The Bible is clear that God has placed a sixth sense in every person and the Influencer that He has sent into this world to guide our sixth sense to the truth is the Holy Spirit. As you will see in future chapters, there are many influences that vie for our sixth sense's attention. We each have to decide to which influence we are going to listen.

1. Romans 2:15 NASB
2. www.biblios.com Greek Interlinear Bible; word study; Strong's concordance. (This is an incredible internet tool, free of charge, designed to help anyone who is interested in studying this great ancient text in more detail.)
3. www.biblios.com Greek interlinear Bible; word study; Strong's concordance.

THE JOURNEY REVEALED - CHPT 2

We are all individuals on a journey of life together. We are all going about it differently. I am one of those individuals, at heart, that believes we could all get along if we just discovered the truth and agreed to disagree while we are searching.

Let me give you another illustration to start this chapter out:

Human beings have really made a mess out of things. We have been fighting over who is right and who is wrong for millennia. There must be truth in here somewhere. We must be guided to our higher power somehow. As the picture illustrates, there are many perceived roads to the higher power. From this point forward we will call our higher power God.

Depending upon our culture and upbringing, we may more readily fall into one way of thought over another. Some choose Buddhism, Islam, Hinduism, Christianity, or Judaism, and the list could go on and on. Some people would say that they are all acceptable means to God. However, if we studied each of the path's teachers, we would find that many of them will not acknowledge this type of acceptance. Because of the lack of agreement, we are left asking ourselves whose way is the right way to get across the divide of our humanity?

Think of your own journey thus far. Think of all the influences, both good and bad, that have led you to your understanding of God, or your "higher power." You have a chosen response or you are in the process of choosing, but the reality is that culture, family, experience, and even education have influenced us all.

You may disagree with some of the information shared from this point forward, but please keep reading and see if it makes sense to your journey.

We all listen to our sixth sense differently. We have the freedom to choose what we are going to believe to be true about God—or if we even believe there is a God. If there is a right answer in this search, then I want to know I have chosen correctly. If I am wrong, there might be some consequences that I don't like.

I do not want to argue about which "religion" or which "way of thought" is right or wrong. I simply want to help you discover the way to your higher power. From this point forward only the Holy Spirit can guide your sixth sense to truth. All I will say about every other option is that they are competing for your attention, and in the end, if you choose incorrectly, you will be disappointed. Most religions have some type of truth in them, or they wouldn't be so believable. What we will find in later chapters is these other religions get us started on our journey towards god, but only one of them can complete the journey to God.

Our sixth sense is compelling us to figure out how to get to God, and we will be discussing how to listen to this sixth sense accurately. Remember, magic can trick our other senses, yet with a little explanation we can come to a proper understanding. Our sixth sense can be tricked into believing certain things are true, yet with a little explanation we can keep our sixth sense from being deceived.

OUR PERSONAL GUIDE - CHPT 3

Let's take a moment to understand our sixth sense. Early on in our journey, the Holy Spirit is at work guiding our sixth sense or our "conscience" to our higher power. The Holy Spirit is guiding us to the only way to get to the higher power which is through Jesus Christ.

Let me encourage you with my incredible artwork. This is a new picture that we are going to use:

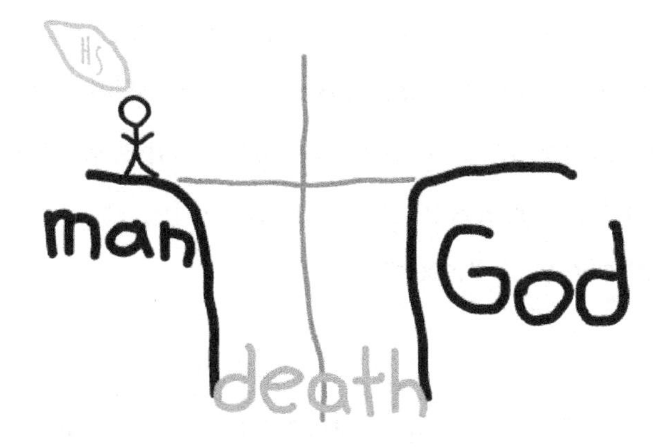

That great ancient text, the Bible, has something to say about this picture too.

> *Jesus said to him, "I am the way, and the Truth, and the life; no one comes to the Father but through Me."* John 14:6 NASB

By Jesus' own definition, He is the one that makes becoming a Christ follower exclusive. According to Jesus, anyone that preaches or teaches another way is a deceiver trying to trick your sixth sense. Only Jesus provides safe passage to God. That is the ultimate truth that the Holy Spirit is trying to guide your sixth sense to. Whether you accept that belief is up to you, but I hope to shed light on how your journey can look if you choose to listen to the Holy Spirit.

According to the picture, man is on one side of a chasm, God is on the other side of the chasm, and at the bottom of the chasm is death. According to Jesus, if we choose any other path across that chasm, we die. That is why he doesn't want us to be deceived. According to Jesus, the only way across that divide is through Him.

If we truly want to cross that chasm of death, if we genuinely want to hear what our sixth sense is telling us, then we must yield to the teachings of Jesus Christ as he leads us to God.

> *I am astonished that you are so quickly deserting the one who called you by the grace of Christ and are turning to a different gospel—which is really no gospel at all. Evidently some people are throwing you into confusion and are trying to pervert the gospel of Christ.* ***But even if we or an angel from***

> ***heaven should preach a gospel other than the one we preached to you, let him be eternally condemned!*** *As we have already said, so now I say again: If anybody is preaching to you a gospel other than what you accepted, let him be eternally condemned!* Galatians 1:6-9

When the Holy Spirit inspired men to write the word of God, He knew people were going to try to pervert the gospel. Gospel means good news, and it was good news to hear that humans could commune with God and have a relationship with Him. The Holy Spirit knew there were going to be many deceivers who will come and try to trick people out of believing in Jesus Christ. He wrote it down in the Bible, so we wouldn't be deceived. According to the Bible, and the Holy Spirit if you believe that there is any other way to get to God, then you are being tricked.

> *All Scripture is God-breathed and is useful for teaching, rebuking, correcting and training in righteousness.* 2 Timothy 3:16

This passage is very important to understand as we think about the picture at the beginning of this chapter. As we are all on this journey of discovering God, the voice that we need to learn to identify to guide our sixth sense is the Holy Spirit.

The Holy Spirit is constantly available to guide us to the truth. There are many distractions that vie for our attention along the way, but the Holy Spirit is right there trying to guide our sixth sense to the truth. It is our job to learn how to listen. As we read in 2 Timothy, the Scripture is God breathed. The Greek word for "breathed" is *pneó* meaning- to blow, breathe, as the wind.

A similar passage that describes the process of the Holy Spirit in relationship to the word of God is found in 2 Peter:

> *For prophecy never had its origin in the will of man, but men spoke from God as they were carried along by the Holy Spirit.* 2 Peter 1:21

What these two passages are saying is that the Holy Spirit wrote the word of God. The Holy Spirit is the breath of God. If you really want to know what the Holy Spirit is saying, then you must learn the Scriptures.

The Holy Spirit is the one who guided as man wrote the Word. As we learn to listen to our inner conscience, we must realize that the Holy Spirit is never going to go against what the scriptures has said is true. I hear so many Christ-followers and even non-Christ followers longing to hear some direct word from God. They want some divine intervention. Let me assure you that until you know the Word of God more intimately, even if you do receive one of those supernatural experiences, you will probably mess up the meaning or interpretation because you won't know how to use the information considering scripture.

I realized this truth the first time when I was fourteen years old. My dad was dying of cancer and we had some friends that were praying and prophesying messages of healing over my dad. Messages that they had received in a vision or a direct word from the Holy Spirit.

A couple of weeks later my dad died. As I was in the stairwell of Hillsdale Community Health Center crying and reminding God of the vision that had been given, the Holy Spirit clearly spoke to me and said, "Son, I did give that lady the vision, and I did heal your dad, and I was preparing him for his healing. But I was preparing him for his eternal healing not his earthly healing. That lady just interpreted the vision incorrectly." At that moment, at age fourteen, I realized that man's desire to believe what we want to believe gets in the way of the truth of what the Holy Spirit is really saying to us.

Here is what you must take away from this chapter before reading on: God is calling all men to himself. He paved the way to get to him by sending Jesus to show us the way. Upon Jesus' exit from this world, He sent the Holy Spirit to continually prompt us toward God's calling, and give us power to differentiate between Truth and fiction when it comes to religion, but man screws up His message.

You may have noticed I use the term "Christ-follower." I want you to understand that what I am speaking of in this book will lead you to a very personal relationship with the God of this universe. If I use the word "Christian" or "Christianity," you may potentially think of some religion that has a history of wrongdoing in its past. Many people claim to follow Christianity without ever following Christ, and it is my greatest desire to see that come to an end.

In the next four chapters, we are going to discuss the way many people try to live out this relationship without listening to the Holy Spirit. These next four chapters are not healthy ways of living, nor are they our desired end, but you can decide for yourself if you think they are wise ways of living.

NOT ENOUGH - CHPT 4

This chapter makes me very sad to write. The number of people who have lived their lives in this state of relationship will someday truly be revealed and determined by God, not man. However, the Holy Spirit wrote about this way of living, and warned us not to live like this. The Holy Spirit wouldn't have warned us about this way of thinking and living if it wasn't going to happen.

Let me draw you a picture of the type of relationship with Christ that this chapter will be talking about:

The Bible says that there will be many who acknowledge Jesus with their lips. They tell others about Jesus and even do great things in His name, yet somehow they don't take hold of the truth of a relationship with Christ.

> *Not everyone who says to Me, "Lord, Lord!" will enter the kingdom of heaven, but [only] the one who does the will of My Father in heaven. On that day many will say to Me, "Lord, Lord, didn't we prophesy in Your name, drive out demons in Your name, and do many miracles in Your name?"* Matthew 7:21-22 HCSB

Many people argue about how this really happens or what it even looks like; my concern is that I don't want it to be you.

To acknowledge Jesus with your lips is not enough. We must do more than that. It must become a part of who we are. We must begin to walk across the bridge acknowledging and doing what He has told us in His Word; the Word that was written by the Holy Spirit.

Again the Word of God says,

> *My dear children, I write this to you so that you will not sin. But if anybody does sin, we have one who speaks to the Father in our defense—Jesus Christ, the Righteous One. He is the atoning sacrifice for*

> *our sins, and not only for ours but also for the sins of the whole world.* 1 John 2:1-2

This passage clearly identifies that Jesus is still the only way to get to God. It identifies for us that if we sin (which we need to know that we have and that we will), Jesus is the reason we can keep moving toward God. He doesn't make this path to God possible just for you and me; He did this for the whole world to be saved. This passage in 1 John continues to explain how this relationship must work:

> *We know that we have come to know him if we obey his commands.* 1 John 2:3

Just telling others about Jesus is not enough. Just saying that He is the way is not enough; we must know and obey Him. Obedience to Christ's way of living is what will identify us as true Christ-followers. The passage goes on:

> *The man who says, "I know him," but does not do what he commands is a liar, and the truth is not in him.* 1 John 2:4

The Holy Spirit knew that this idea of being a follower of Jesus and just talking about Jesus was going to cause a lot of people frustration, so he put this passage in Scripture for us to read and live our lives by. If we do not walk in obedience, then we don't really know him. The Truth is Jesus. The Truth, however, is often perverted by our own desires. The Truth, Jesus, is not a part of us if we are standing at the beginning of the cross as illustrated in the picture just talking about Jesus being the way without following him with our lives. Look at this next verse:

> *But if anyone obeys his word, God's love is truly made complete in him. This is how we know we are in him:* ***Whoever claims to live in him must walk as Jesus did.*** 1 John 2:5-6

Did you read that? The only one that is truly in Christ is the one who is walking as Jesus walked. How do we ever stand a chance of walking as Jesus walked? It is when we learn to live by the Holy Spirit, speaking to and guiding our sixth sense. Our sixth sense knows there is a better way to live. It is tempted by all kinds of teachings, but the Holy Spirit can guide our sixth sense away from deceit.

There are many people that think it is impossible to live as Jesus lived. It is not. God would not command us to do something if it were impossible. He wouldn't tell us our whole future in eternity depends upon this very act and then take away the possibility. Rather, this seeming impossibility is the very reason we have the Holy Spirit here to guide us along. That is why we have the Bible to give us instruction.

Maybe this is you. Maybe you find yourself standing on the sideline pointing and saying, "Yeah, Jesus is the way," but you have never taken the walk across the cross. If this is you then it is time to acknowledge where you truly stand on the bridge of faith, so you can start making it right.

> *Not everyone who says to me, "Lord, Lord," will enter the kingdom of heaven, but only he who does the will of my Father who is in heaven. Many will say to me on that day, "Lord, Lord, did we not prophesy in your name, and in your name drive out demons and perform many miracles?" Then I will tell them plainly, "I never knew you. Away from me, you evildoers!"* Matthew 7:21-23

Don't let this passage be a description of you and your life. Don't let this chapter be a description of your understanding of Jesus. You are so close to the truth. Jesus is trying to warn us that there are many who are still standing on the wrong side of the great chasm. There are many who are saying He is the way to get across, yet many still will not do what He wills. How do we learn what He wills? By bringing our sixth sense into obedience to the Holy Spirit's guidance. We do this by walking across the cross of Christ. Then, we try to live in this world the way Christ lived.

You might still be saying, "That is impossible!" It is true that even while walking the cross of Christ you will still sin and stumble. However, the reality is, as you walk in His steps, the sin will become less and less through the guidance of the Holy Spirit. There is so much more. Keep on reading.

DECEIVED - CHPT 5

We discussed the first unhealthy way that some people try to follow Christ. Now let us define the second unhealthy way. Some who say they follow Christ try to have one foot on the cross while keeping one foot firmly established in the world. You may find that this next phase of the walk is you. You have listened to the Holy Spirit, you want to do what he says, and you know Jesus is the way, but there are some things that you aren't willing to let go.

Let me show you another picture.

In this picture, you have one foot on the bridge, but are not willing to put your whole weight on the bridge. We want to take that walk across the bridge. We want to believe that Christ has saved us from sin and death, but there are some things that are really enticing in life. There are some things that are just too "fun." In fact, they are the very things that have defined who we are. They are the very things that guide our behavior and decisions. They are the very things that define our friendships and our relationships. Many times, they are also the very things that you must let go.

You can't live in both worlds. Some preachers will say that you can. You will soon see that God's Word says that you can't. If this chapter reflects you and your behavior, and you are trying to live with one foot in your old ways and with on foot on the cross, then you have probably experienced a conflicted conscience at times or you have created a justification for your behavior. You may even live a life of extreme guilt and self-condemnation.

You see, the Holy Spirit is trying to guide your sixth sense into giving these things up. Unfortunately, because these lifestyle choices are so ingrained in your life, it just doesn't feel normal to try and change, so you attempt to make excuses for your actions and behavior. Many people even find a church that will tell them what they want to hear, so it helps them justify their life. After all, finding a church that condones our actions helps our sixth sense be quiet for a while. Remember how magic can trick our senses? We can also appease or trick our sixth sense if we give it false information long enough.

Many people think that this appeasement phenomenon is unique to our time and culture. There are several sins that people have been trying to justify for thousands of years. We are no different than those who were early followers of Christ. Again, let's look at the Bible, the Word of God, which is written by the Holy Spirit, the voice that is trying to lead our sixth sense to the truth. Let's see how the Holy Spirit has tried to guide Christ followers to the truth:

> *Do you not know that the wicked will not inherit the kingdom of God? Do not be deceived: Neither the sexually immoral nor idolaters nor adulterers nor male prostitutes nor homosexual offenders nor thieves nor the greedy nor drunkards nor slanderers nor swindlers will inherit the kingdom of God.* [11] *And that is what some of you were. But you were washed, you were sanctified, you were justified in the name of the Lord Jesus Christ and by the Spirit of our God.* 1 Corinthians 6:9-11

Holy shnikies! Do you see that? The Holy Spirit is telling us to get off the crack. Don't be deceived. Your old ways are deceiving you. This business of trying to live in two worlds has been going on since the days of early Christ followers.

Let me break down this passage by defining how these behaviors try to lull our sixth sense asleep. Let me try to help you see how these behaviors have been a stumbling block for thousands of years.

Sexually immoral – That is anyone that thinks of any sexual act outside the confines of the marriage bed. Sex is not bad. God devoted a whole book of the Bible to talk about the marriage relationship. He even told us to climb our palm trees and take hold of its fruit. Read the book of Song of Solomon if you are unaware of this symbolism. Sex is a very good thing in the proper context.

The Bible goes on to identify that any sexual immorality is strictly forbidden. Pornography, adultery, lust, bestiality, incest, rape … all of it is immoral. (If you think pornography is new to our culture, study art and the historical cultures.)

Paul is the accepted author of the Book of Corinthians and he is identifying the same problems that we have in the 21st century. Paul was talking to those who were in the church. They liked their sin too. Their sin defined them and who they were! Paul said, "NO!" It is not proper for a person who is following the way of Christ. If you think it is ok to sin sexually in any manner, you have tricked your sixth sense into believing a lie.

If you think any of the sins that were listed in this passage are ok, then you are just like the early church and you are trying to justify your behavior and you are being deceived.

Paul very kindly gives us a list of sins that people have struggled with since the beginning. Remember this is the same list the early Christ followers were reverting to. This wasn't written recently. This list of sins deceived even the first Christ followers into thinking they were "okay." Paul is begging his audience, and all future audiences, to stop being deceived. Let's see what else has been tripping people up for years.

Idolaters – Idolatry can be defined as anything that is more important than Christ. Is there anything in your life more important than Christ? It could be a literal idol. Maybe you come from a satanic worship background or a new age background and you cherish your relics, stones, or gems. Maybe you come from a Buddhist background, and you have your little shrines in your home to keep in touch with your heritage and ancestors. Maybe you have your money that no one can touch, or your collection of treasures. Your family may even come before your walk with Christ. According to the Corinthians passage, we need to be aware that absolutely nothing can be in front of following Christ.

Adulterers – If you think that it is okay to sleep with anyone that you have not entered a marriage relationship with, you are an adulterer. In fact, Christ went so far as to say if you think lustfully after another person, you are an adulterer. The Holy Spirit, through the Bible, is specifically saying that these things are not acceptable for a Christ follower.

Male Prostitutes – Some people think that prostitution is a new phenomenon, but it has been going on for millennia. It is not becoming of a Christian. I don't care if it is how you make money to pay the bills; it is not right. Let the Holy Spirit lead you to a new way.

Homosexual offenders – Here goes the Bible being all politically incorrect again. If you attend a church that suggests that homosexuality is okay and is condoned biblically, you are deceiving your sixth sense into believing a lie.

I want to pause for a second and speak to those who are beginning to think, “This is the most pointless journey ever. I can never truly give up these things.” I am not suggesting that if you listen to the Holy Spirit guide your sixth sense that you will never be tempted to want to sin again. I would be a liar if I told you that. What I am trying to identify is the idea that it is okay if we want to continue to live in sin. The message of Christ is that He died to deliver us from sin. I am not saying that we will never mess up. I want to communicate that if you really want your sixth sense to be guided to truth, then you must desire a life of purity and not of sin.

The picture at the beginning of this chapter is a direct reflection of what I am talking about. I have counseled hundreds of people. Many of them are stuck at this step. They like their sin too much. You cannot get both feet on the cross unless you are willing to acknowledge that what you are trying to hold on to is impure, ungodly, and unbiblical.

The word of God has warned us about this battle. Unfortunately, many pastors across the globe are condoning this unhealthy position in Christ–one foot on the cross and one foot in our old ways. Sadly it just adds to the confusion.

Don't get mad yet. Read this next passage and see what the Holy Spirit is trying to say to your sixth sense:

> *Preach the Word; be prepared in season and out of season; correct, rebuke and encourage—with great patience and careful instruction.* ***For the time will come when men will not put up with sound doctrine****. Instead, to suit their own desires, they will gather around them a great number of teachers to say what their itching ears want to hear.* ***They will turn their ears away from the truth and turn aside to myths.*** 2 Timothy 4:2-4

It breaks my heart that some of you, in order to appease your itching ears, have gone off and found a teacher or a preacher that will tell you what you want to hear. (If you are a pastor and you are reading this and you are one of those ear ticklers, I beg you to change your ways. For the sake of those who follow you, please reconsider your teachings.)

Let's keep reading the list. The list is far more pervasive than just our sexually deviant behavior. It has to do with many more lifestyles.

Thieves – white collar or blue collar. All theft is a sin. None of it is justifiable. If you take anything that is not yours, it is theft. In the ancient world, it was very common to use scales to measure goods. Many times, they would use imbalanced scales to short change people. That was thievery. Throughout all the scriptures, God comes down hard on those who use dishonesty as a means to personal gain. The Bible even uses the illustration of not giving the correct amount of money back to God as a form of stealing. Whether you steal stamps from the office or millions from the wealthy, thievery is not acceptable for a Christ follower.

Greedy – Our modern banking system and credit card companies are in gross error of the scriptures. So are many who are in key governmental positions around the world. Greed creeps into our lives in crafty little ways. If you get offended when money is talked about at church, or if you get annoyed by those who ask for money by the roadside, or if you have the ability to help others less fortunate than you and you don't, there is a strong probability that you suffer from greed.

Drunks – I am not against drinking, but the Scripture is clear that drunkenness is not acceptable. All of you who like to party on the weekend, college students who are trying to fit in, high school students who are going to church on Sunday after getting hammered on the weekend, moms and dads who are trying to drink your pain away; you are living in sin and you are being deceived.

Slanderers – Have you ever lied about someone? Have you ever let someone say something bad about another person because you were mad at them? You could have defended them, but you didn't because they deserved it. You have slandered and allowed another person to be slandered. If you ever lied, you are a slanderer. It is not okay. It is a sin. It is a sin.

Swindlers – A swindler is a person who sells an item or a concept that is faulty by design, or sells a product to a consumer who has no need and cannot afford it. For example, you are a swindler when you sell used cars that you know are pieces of junk and you purposely deceive people until you get what you want. Please find a new job if you feel you need to lie or deceive others, or at least start being honest. God will honor you if you would follow His Word.

Did you catch all that Paul wrote in this passage? It sounds like he was living with us today. Notice too that Paul was equally displeased with the lying gossip as he was the homosexual offender. Deceptive sin covers far more territory than just sexual behaviors.

Please do not deceive yourself any longer into thinking that any of these things are ok. I am not talking to those of you who are desperately trying not to sin yet seem to keep messing up and giving into temptation. I am talking to the countless millions who have given up on trying and no longer call their actions sinful. If you are really trying to live like the Holy Spirit desires you to live, then you will try to follow Christ's example.

Lord, if there is anyone reading this book that is trying to live in both worlds right now, I ask through the power of your Holy Spirit that they will acknowledge their sin, repent, and turn from whatever sin is on that list. Lord, guide them to your truth and help them to stop lying to themselves. Amen.

If we want to walk in Christ's steps, if we want to try to live by the Holy Spirit, if we want to try to live the way this book suggests, then we have to understand that sin is not acceptable. We must be torn up over our deliberate desire to sin. We must be sad that it is because of our sin that Jesus even had to come down to Earth in the first place. We have to accept that He did all that He did to show us a better way of life and, that he has provided a way to live a new life. Keeping one foot in our old ways and one foot on the cross will only lead to disaster.

FOOLISHNESS - CHPT 6

This next chapter is for all those immature individuals out there that think this is a game. The word of God, in the book of Proverbs, calls this next type of behavior the behavior of fools. This chapter addresses the balance of God's grace for those who have trusted in Christ and how unhealthy it is to deliberately abuse God's grace.

I have not found too many people that like to be called a fool, so hopefully you don't find yourself relating to this chapter. Unfortunately, this is the chapter that I have some personal experience in, and I am here to tell you this next chapter is a bad way to live. You are definitely not living according to Christ's example if you are doing what this chapter addresses.

To get us started, let me impress you with my artistic skills once more.

Imagine that little stick figure is jumping up and down out there on the cross. This chapter is for those of you who have decided to follow Christ. You know He is the way and you even genuinely try to follow Him—sometimes. You even genuinely repent—sometimes. You even genuinely feel bad about your sin—sometimes.

Then life hits you square between the eyes. Maybe your sixth sense gets tricked into believing some lie that sounded really good. You may have even gotten to the point where you are experiencing God's grace at a whole new level. You see, this foolish behavior gets you to the point where you start taking advantage of God's grace. You begin to experience the security and the strength that the cross of Christ represents. The problem, if you choose to live in this behavior, is that you will begin to suffer the punishment of the Holy Spirit or His behavior modification process.

The really good news is that the cross of Christ can stand up under the weight of all sin; that is the whole purpose of the cross. However, it is not there so that God's children can make a mockery of His grace. When Christ followers get to this point in their walk with God, they get to experience the Holy Spirit at a whole new level.

Take a look at some of these next passages of scripture to see what I mean:

> *"Everything is permissible"—but not everything is beneficial. "Everything is permissible"—but not everything is constructive.* 1 Corinthians 10:23

Some people who are on their journey to God will look at a verse like this and think, "Okay, then I am secure in my walk to God. I am allowed to do anything I want because I have already been saved." A person living in this type of lifestyle is failing to understand what "not everything is beneficial" means. While they might be jumping around on the cross experiencing grace and a new freedom that they have never experienced before, they are making a mockery of what Christ came to do.

Remember why we started our journey on the cross? We were led to the truth of Christ by our sixth sense. Our sixth sense is now subject to the Holy Spirit. Remember once we have accepted the way of Christ, the Holy Spirit is what guides us to Truth. Before we accepted Christ, the Holy Spirit was calling to our sixth sense, after Christ, the Holy Spirit is responsible for directing and guiding our sixth sense. Look at what the Holy Spirit wrote through man in the text of the Scriptures:

> *What shall we say, then? Shall we go on sinning so that grace may increase? By no means! We died to sin; how can we live in it any longer?* Romans 6:1-2

What the Holy Spirit is saying to you is that if you have genuinely accepted what the cross has done for you, then you won't go out there living however you want to live, abusing Christ's sacrifice. This passage of Scripture is here to remind us that even though the cross is strong enough to handle and forgive us of any sin we can imagine, that sin is who we were, and if we don't stop sinning or jumping on the grace of Christ, things are going to get unpleasant. Or as the NIV says, "things will no longer be beneficial."

Let me show you what happens to those who choose to abuse the grace of Christ. It is a good thing the Holy Spirit saw this potential abuse coming when He wrote the Bible.

And do not grieve the Holy Spirit of God, with whom you were sealed for the day of redemption.
Ephesians 4:29-30

The whole passage is talking about how we are supposed to live our lives as we walk across the cross of Christ. In the middle of the instruction this verse is given as a warning. In other words, the whole book of Ephesians tells us how to live and that if we don't do what it says, then we are grieving the Holy Spirit. We are literally grieving the guide of our sixth sense.

The warning isn't "don't grieve God the Father in heaven." There is no warning here about "wait until your father gets home." There is no warning that if we keep jumping on the grace of Jesus Christ that the cross will get weak and we will plummet to our death. There is no warning about "don't live contrary to this passage because you are really going to make Jesus sad or even mad."

The warning is clear: don't grieve the Holy Spirit. Why? Because the Holy Spirit is guiding your sixth sense, that sense that is supposed to be learning how not to be deceived. The Holy Spirit wrote the Word of God, so He is saying, "You really don't want to keep living in a way that is contrary to my Word."

You might be an unbeliever saying to yourself, "Who cares, the Bible is just some book that was written over two thousand years ago; what could possibly happen to me today?" Remember, this passage is for those who choose the way of the fool on the cross of Christ. The fool in this instance is the person who has chosen Christ, and is ignoring the Holy Spirits clear direction in the word of God. Our sixth sense is saying, "Don't live like this. It is a bad idea."

Again, the Holy Spirit knew He was going to have to address our ignorant behavior more than once, so He words His warning a little differently in another passage. Check this one out:

> *Then Peter said, 'Ananias, how is it that Satan has so filled your heart that you have lied to the Holy Spirit and have kept for yourself some of the money you received for the land? Didn't it belong to you before it was sold? And after it was sold, wasn't the money at your disposal? What made you think of doing such a thing? You have not lied to men but to God.' When Ananias heard this, he fell down and died. And great fear seized all who heard what had*

> *happened.* Acts 5:3-5

This is an amazing story of a man and his wife who chose to lie to the Holy Spirit. Peter didn't ask Ananias, "Why did you lie to God the Father?" He didn't ask, "Why did you lie to God the Son?" He said, "How is it that you have lied to (God) the Holy Spirit?" This passage is suggesting that through the Holy Spirit, Ananias' sixth sense had been telling him his decision-making process was a bad idea. Ananias and his wife had deliberately sold a parcel of land and said that they were giving all the money to the church. However, they decided to keep some of the money for themselves. They were lying, they were greedy, and they were being swindlers. Yet Ananias went ahead with their decision and he died.

Wow! This is New Testament grace, my friends. It is a foolish idea to live contrary to the Holy Spirit's leading. Don't grieve the Holy Spirit! It is a bad idea. He can rock your world. The story goes on:

> *About three hours later his wife came in, not knowing what had happened. Peter asked her, 'Tell me, is this the price you and Ananias got for the land?' 'Yes,' she said, 'that is the price.' Peter said to her, 'How could you agree to test the Spirit of the*

> *Lord? Look! The feet of the men who buried your husband are at the door, and they will carry you out also.' At that moment she fell down at his feet and died. Then the young men came in and, finding her dead, carried her out and buried her beside her husband. Great fear seized the whole church and all who heard about these events."* Acts 5:7-11

Peter gave the wife, Saphira, a chance to come clean. She refused. She stuck with her un-repentance, jumping on the grace of Jesus—defiant behavior—and she lied to the Holy Spirit. Peter said, "How could you agree to test the Spirit of the Lord?"

Look at the results. She drops dead too. God's Word, the Holy Spirit, says, "Great fear seized the whole church and all who heard about these events." I wonder if it causes any fear in you. It should. Are you living foolishly? Are you living in total contradiction to what you know is right according to your sixth sense? If so, let me tell you plainly, you are living a fool's life. Don't keep grieving the Holy Spirit. It is not going to work out well for you.

I have been in ministry now for over 20 years, and I know that most people reject this type of warning. Most people refuse to think that their sin is really that bad. Many choose to continue to do what they feel like doing. Let me give a personal example of my behavior that lead me into the Holy Spirit's discipline.

I was 18 years old and completing my first year of college. I was planning on transferring from Jackson Community College in the fall to play football for Taylor University. My dream of playing football was about to come true. Many people thought I was crazy since I had never played football in my life, but I was convinced I could do it. Taylor was not cutting anybody that year in order to rebuild the program. (That was my only way in.) I knew that I was called into the ministry. I was even registered for all the ministry classes. But I can assure you in my heart of hearts, I was not going to Taylor to enter the ministry. I was going to go play football. Football had become my idol—my god. I was putting sports before God.

In March of 1992, this 18 year old ended up with twisted gut disease. I was in a drug-induced coma for three days; I almost died. I woke up wearing a colostomy bag and being told I wouldn't be playing sports again. I was in the hospital for three weeks, and then I was at home for another month recovering from my ordeal.

One excruciatingly painful night, the Holy Spirit began to deal with me through the Word. The book of James chapter four rocked my world. In short, the Lord simply told me, "Who are you to say that you are going to go to Taylor and play football. Your life is a mist, here today, gone tomorrow. Instead you should have said, Lord willing."

I immediately repented, I asked God to forgive me for my mixed-up priorities, and I promised Him I would go to whatever college he wanted me to go to and that I didn't have to play football. I simply asked him to make it really clear to me what school he wanted me to go to. I asked him to have a letter in the mail in the morning from the college of His choice. As soon as I prayed that prayer, my pain immediately went away and I was able to go to sleep.

The next day I got a letter from a school 600 miles away, in a state I had never visited, from a school I had never even heard of, Northwestern Christian College. I didn't waste any time in transferring my credits and completing the application process. I made sure my major was Pastoral Studies. The story gets even better. My colostomy bag was temporary. The doctors were wrong about me never being able to play sports, and Northwestern had a football team that wasn't cutting anybody. With 4 ½ months of recovery, I was playing collegiate football by August. Praise the Lord.

I am a living testimony that the Holy Spirit doesn't want to be a downer, but He will be sure that we keep our focus on God first.

Trust me, the Holy Spirit takes offense or is grieved by deliberate foolish behavior.

I will tell you one story of my wife. We had gone through a very difficult patch of ministry, and I and the Lord had encouraged her not to say anything. Let it go. It doesn't matter what people say or think about us. It is not our job to vindicate or defend ourselves. Let time reveal the truth. She proceeded to do her own thing. Within less than half an hour, she became violently ill. As soon as she repented, she was better. The Holy Spirit does not tolerate disobedient behavior.

If you still struggle with this idea that the Holy Spirit punishes us, let me give you one more passage of Scripture. The Holy Spirit takes great offense at Christians who choose to live disobediently and take advantage of the strength of the cross of Christ.

> *Therefore, whoever eats the bread or drinks the cup of the Lord in an unworthy manner will be guilty of sinning against the body and blood of the Lord. A man ought to examine himself before he eats of the bread and drinks of the cup. For anyone who eats and drinks without recognizing the body of the Lord eats and* ***drinks judgment on himself****. That is why many among you are weak and sick, and a number of you have fallen asleep. But if we judged ourselves, we would not come under judgment.* ***When we are judged by the Lord, we are being disciplined so that we will not be condemned with the world****.* 1 Corinthians 11:27-32

I beg you to honestly look at your life. Judge your attitude and your actions. Look at your heart. I have had so many people come into my office wondering why their lives are falling apart, how God could allow these things to be happening. You fill in the blank for what these things are. The problem is that nobody likes to accept that maybe they are happening because they are grieving the Holy Spirit. We must properly examine our way of life as we acknowledge what Christ did for us on the cross.

Let me give you one more personal example. I was 20 years old. I was in a semi-serious relationship with my girlfriend, and she was going to go on our family vacation with us. We were pure in our relationship, yet if I am honest with myself I was hoping that things might lend themselves to "fun" behavior.

Less than 12 hours before we were scheduled to leave for our vacation, I broke my leg severely. I was playing backyard football and broke my tibia and fibula. When I lifted my leg up, my lower leg fell to the ground. It was a bad break. I ended up in the hospital with a double fracture and was told I wouldn't be able to walk on it for six months. Crutches for six months!?

I was 20 years old; this was not in my plans. I was going on vacation, and I also had a mission trip I was supposed to go on in July. This happened at the end of May. I ended up with double pneumonia and an extended stay in the Lutheran Hospital in Ft. Wayne, Indiana.

While lying on my back (again… I am a slow learner), God clearly spoke to me and said, "When are you going to learn?" I quickly repented. This time I had impure motives.

He didn't need to spell it out for me. After repenting, I was walking on my leg in two weeks. The doctor said he had never seen a bone heal so fast in all his life. As God is my witness, I looked right at him and told him it was because God healed me. I went on my mission trip in the end of July, and never once had to use my crutches after those first two weeks.

I repented and stopped jumping on the grace of Christ. I knew God's grace was sufficient, but He didn't want me even thinking about sin. Some people still try to convince me that God doesn't work this way, but I know that my God loves me and He has had to discipline me. I have so many more stories that I could share. I simply ask that you look at your life and examine it closely to see if God is trying or has tried to get your attention. I could tell of times where my car has broken down, plumbing has sprung leaks, house wiring has gone bad, all in direct correlation to my decisions. How do I know? Because as soon as I repented, the situation was corrected. As has happened in my life and as we read in the scriptures, if an affliction or trial comes from the Lord, there is healing and relief in repentance.

> *Therefore confess your sins to each other and pray for each other so that you may be healed. The prayer of a righteous person is powerful and effective.* James 5:16

There are times when bad things have certainly happened that were not as a result of discipline, but because I walk closely with the Holy Spirit, I know when those times are. The question is, do you know the difference?

If you choose to continue to live in deliberate sin, then please don't get mad at God when your life turns to crap. You are grieving the Holy Spirit. This is not rocket science. Things are not beneficial for you because you are not listening to the Holy Spirit's true voice as He guides your sixth sense.

By this point, I hope you are beginning to learn that the Word of God, the Bible, should be playing a large part in understanding the Holy Spirit. I have given you an example of God's corrective love in moments of adulterous thoughts, greedy decisions, and idolatrous behavior, and those are just examples out of an aspiring pastor. I have also given an example of my wife's slanderous behavior. The good news is that during all correction, God's grace is great and sufficient. He forgives us beyond all measure. He holds no grudges, but He does call us to grow in maturity.

I hope you really understand this chapter because grieving the Holy Spirit and living foolish, deliberate, sinful lifestyles keep a lot of people from ever reaching the goal that God the Father has for them. It is time to move on to the fourth and final inappropriate response to the Holy Spirit.

FRUSTRATED - CHPT 7

This next chapter can be the most frustrating of all chapters, because it has to do with complete surrender. Let me give you a word of encouragement at this point: I have experienced every chapter of this book that I have shared with you. Maybe you can relate or maybe you were smart enough to avoid some of the pitfalls I have experienced. I have found that many you reach this next stage get frustrated with their walk with the Holy spirit. Once you reach this stage, you are so close. Now is not the time to give up. If this chapter reflects your walk with Christ, then feeling like giving up is an ever-present reality at this point of your journey. The desire to give up is partly why this stage is so frustrating.

Let me show you a picture of what this part of the journey looks like. As you look at this picture, remember that we are trying to get this little stick figure across the great divide. We want to get to the point where we walk in step with the Holy Spirit, or shall we say on the solid ground with God.

If you are at this point of your spiritual journey understanding the role of the Holy Spirit and how He directs and shapes your sixth sense, my heart goes out to you. Getting past this point took me until I was forty-one years old. I pray that my struggles will expedite your understanding of your sixth sense. I personally found this to be the most painful stage to go through; however, it was absolutely critical that I went through it. If it had not been for the last nine years of my life and ministry, this book would never have been born. I pray that you can benefit greatly from what is shared.

This is the stage of life where we don't abuse the grace of Christ. We do live our lives in obedience, and we can see all that Christ has done for us. We can see all that God has in store for us; we have heard from the Holy Spirit before and we have walked and talked with Him, but there is still something missing.

There is a great story in the Old Testament about a group of people called the Israelites, God's chosen people. All of creation, all of the Scriptures, everything that I am talking about here in this book is made possible through God's interaction with this people group. Part of this relationship that God has with the Jewish nation goes back to this amazing story where God delivered these stubborn, self-righteous, stiff-necked, foolish-living people out of captivity. But they wanted to go back to their captive land because at least they knew what they had there. They were always whining to God about what they had to go through.

The journey was to their promised land. Just like us in this chapter, they got to the point where they got to look at all that God had in store for them. But there was one giant step remaining: they had to defeat their greatest enemies, they had to fight their greatest fight, and they had to ensure total surrender of their foes. They had to trust that God would deliver them into the promised land.

(I am not going to tell the whole story; you can read it for yourself. It starts in Genesis and ends in Joshua. It is a great representation of what I am talking about here.) The Israelites were not permitted to enter their promised land until they defeated their worst enemy.

The first time they got to this point they chickened out. They got scared and then they were cursed to wander in the wilderness for forty years, until all the leaders that gave way to their fears died out— all but two of them. The two that remained went on to lead a great army and a nation into the very promises of God.

In order to take this final step of getting where God so desperately wants all of his children. In order to get to the point where we walk and talk with him at a level of inexplicable peace, love, joy, contentment, victory, and purposeful living. You must rid yourself of you. You must find your biggest giant; you must face your biggest fears and surrender them totally. If you don't, you will continue to live in the wilderness of your journey, always able to see what God has in store for your life, but never quite reaching it.

So many people want to live by a list of black and white rules, they want a clear understanding of saved and unsaved, I am a Christ follower I am not a Christ follower. This book is not about any of that. It is all about learning to walk in tune with the Holy Spirt. It is all about learning to walk in relationship with God as he guides your sixth sense. It is all about walking in relationship with the Holy Spirit.

Like I said, I lived this way for forty years. It is almost uncanny that my life stage so closely related to that of the Israelites. I wrote the original draft of this book five years ago, but I could never finish it. Those who were first to read and edit the copy marked in the margins that it needed something. It needed an example. I couldn't complete the book because God had to take our family through our most current journey.

On December 4, 2012, God was going to begin taking our family on a journey that I never expected. He asked me to give up eight years of serving at a church with some wonderful people: my family and friends. He asked me to give up all my denominational ties (as a pastor that can be very frustrating), he asked me to move to a land that I had no connections, he asked me to give up all acquired influence, and he asked me to uproot my family while my girls were going into 9th, 8th and 7th grade. He asked me to leave my mom behind and trust that he would take care of her. He asked me to start life all over again. It was the most difficult decision that I have ever made.

I had lived a life of scrapping for everything that I have, I had lived life working since I was thirteen years old. I had never gone without a job or moved without a job in twenty-seven years of life. The magnitude of the unknown cannot even begin to be put into words. Quite honestly, God is still giving me the words to this day. After seven months of wrestling with God on our decision, we moved to Charlotte, North Carolina. As you will hear a little later in the book, we (our whole family) had to face fears and trials and battles I could have never known.

Three years after the move, I am elated to say that God's promises are amazing. I am writing this in the midst of trusting Him on more of His promises. I still have not experienced all that He promised, yet I walk in liberty and peace knowing that I have followed his voice and leading.

I can honestly tell you that if I had stayed in Michigan, I would have been in direct disobedience to the very promptings of God, and I and my family would not have experienced the liberating freedoms that He has shown us in the three years. But it took complete surrender on our whole family's part. I cannot praise my wife and three beautiful daughters enough for their faith and trust in God and in me. I can assure you the last year was not easy.

It has been a difficult three years. Holding on to the promises. Not getting discouraged when things don't seem to go the way that God promised. Trusting that he is still guiding when things seem to fall apart. This stage of our journey can seem very frustrating.

If this chapter reflects where you are at in the journey, then there may be one last sin, one last attitude, one last wrong way of thinking, and one last area of your life that you just aren't willing to yield to God's control. It may be something that is perfectly sin-free. It could even be something as noble as your family, your dreams and aspirations of doing great things for God. Until you are willing to properly identify what this last battle is, be prepared to live a life of frustration. Be prepared to wander in the wilderness until you are ready to experience God's promised land of living totally guided by truth.

I know how easy it is to grow content with the thought, "This will be my lot in life. There are too many giants that will have to be faced. I have everything that I deserve." I'll never really be who Christ wants me to be until I die.

Let me tell you that is a lie from the pit of hell. Jesus came to deliver us from that very thought process. I am not saying that you get to get out of a situation; I am saying Christ came to bring you victory in your situation.

Many Christ followers come to this point in the road and say, "This is my life, these things are what define me as a person, my promised land is coming when I die." While all these things are true, people who live like this are selling themselves very short of what God could really do.

The Holy Spirit has not brought you this far on the journey to just let you live in mediocrity. He has a one final step for you: He must discipline you. He must make sure that you are willing to trust everything He says implicitly. It is not that you have to be perfect or that you will be perfect, it is that He needs to know that you will be obedient to Him and what he asks of you. If this does not make sense to you let me humbly suggest that you are not to this step on your journey yet.

When I wrote this book the first time, I was trying to complete this step by being as good as I could be, by being as righteous as I could be, by being willing to sacrifice myself to whatever the ministry may ask of me. I could follow the rules despite detestation for rules; I could discipline myself with the best of them. But I kept falling short. I couldn't figure out what this last step meant.

Complete trust means whatever your giant is, God knows it and His word has a promise to defeat it. I had two giants I didn't even know existed in Christianity: hard work and American pride. Put those two together and the world is your oyster and God is not needed. I had allowed myself to believe that who I was as a person was validated by my ability to outwork and outlast anyone around me. My internal mindset was, "You might be better than me in every way, but I will always outlast you and outwork you." I prided myself on not allowing anything in life to hurt me, break me, hinder me, discourage me, or depress me. I have been through a lot and this mindset ran deep within me for 40+ years. God had an incredible challenge for me to face in moving to North Carolina. My life's savings went away, I was working with three temp agencies and couldn't even get a job at a factory.

I had twenty years of ministry experience and sent out more resumes than you can imagine and never had a phone call. Depression and darkness set in on me in ways I can't begin to describe. I was in my darkest hour. My giant was whether I really trusted that God would provide and take care of my family. Was my identity truly in Him or in my ability to work?

My doubts went way back to when my dad died when I was fourteen years old. I had been doing the work of the man in our house since the age of eleven because my dad was slowly dying of cancer. He taught me to never give up, to never give in, and told me to make sure that I took care of my mom. I promised I would. And there I was forty years old, no job, no home, no ministry, no money, no prospects, nothing but the command of God that said to move. Many people thought I was crazy, and people questioned whether I really heard from God. I thought I was going crazy at times!

Yet during the darkness, God clearly spoke, and the reason I know it was God is because I know His voice. When you are in a relationship with someone you love, you know when they speak to you.

He simply held me in my weakness and He said, "You have been living your life for the last forty years by your earthly father's set of rules; now it is time to see how your heavenly father is going to do things."

The last three years since He said that, He has opened doors that I never could have opened. He has allowed me to be on staff at the best church I have ever ministered in. He has given our family liberty and freedom that we never would have experienced before. He has provided for my mom in ways I never could have, even if I would have worked another full-time job. Our girls have adjusted better than I could have ever dreamed!

The only downside to our move is that these last few years have been filled with some of the most discouraging and most painful years of my life that I have ever gone through in spite of all the blessings. Yet I know we are in complete alignment with Gods will. He continues to guide and shape and discipline me as I walk in liberty with Him. It has taken the unmet promises combined with continued faith and trust over the last few years to experience the freedom and peace defined in this chapter.

As you will see in the next chapter, **God must have your complete surrender, your complete obedience.**

> *Endure hardship as discipline; God is treating you as sons. For what son is not disciplined by his father? If you are not disciplined (and everyone undergoes discipline), then you are illegitimate children and not true sons. Moreover, we have all had human fathers who disciplined us and we respected them for it. How much more should we submit to the Father of our spirits and live! Our fathers disciplined us for a little while as they thought best; but God disciplines us for our good, that we may share in his holiness. [11] No discipline seems pleasant at the time, but painful. Later on, however, it produces a harvest of righteousness and peace for those who have been trained by it. Therefore, strengthen your feeble arms and weak knees. "Make level paths for your feet," so that the lame may not be disabled, but rather healed.*
> Hebrews 12:7-13

I love this passage. As our final destination will be presented in the next chapter, we are on a journey of becoming a "Hebrew" Christ follower, and in order to do that, we must embrace this passage.

Did you notice this phrase in the passage you read? It said, "How much more should we submit to the Father of our spirits."

Do you get it? The Holy Spirit is trying to get us to come into complete surrender to God. I used to think complete surrender was done through discipline, like hard work and discipline; rather, it is done through trust in God's discipline. There is no discipline that seems pleasant, but when you can finally start embracing your discipline instead of fighting it, your life is going to radically change. God is going to allow you to face your fears as many times as He needs to until you learn to trust that His promises are true for you. Your fear is different than mine. But His promises are just as true for you as they are for Mother Teresa or me.

At this point in the journey, the most common phrase I hear is, "How much more do I have to do? How much more do I have to take?" The answer we don't want to hear is God's answer, "However much it is going to take for your complete trust!"

From personal experience, this is a very selfish, deluded, dangerous question to ask. It is driven from our idea that we have somehow possibly become all that God really wants us to be. This is a very arrogant, prideful pedestal to put ourselves on.

Once we learn to identify complete trust, we can identify our fears and apply God's word more quickly. The Israelites spent years driving out their enemies from their lands. Over and over again, God tested their trust with His promises that He would be their deliverer—not their efforts.

This is the beauty of the Holy Spirit. He knows exactly what your spirit—your sixth sense—needs to go through to come into true surrender. The Holy Spirit has been walking with you and guiding you all the way to this point. He knows you intimately. He has traveled with you through every vile and evil thought you have ever had, and He has seen you in your most humble and righteous moments as well. He has been with you every step of the way, and He knows exactly how deeply rooted your pride, arrogance, lust, bitterness, anger, gluttony, or your…really is.

He will do in you whatever it takes to help you have complete dependence upon Him before you are able to take this final step.

When you are experiencing life at this level, everything hurts. You have two directions to go: Finish the battle of self-sufficiency or take your foot off the solid holy rock of God and keep yourself firmly planted on the grace of Christ and just live there until you die. It is confusing to have one foot in the Promised Land of true liberty and one foot on the grace of Christ and the promise of sufficiency in the wilderness.

I lived forty years here. I thought my step into the promised land was cleaner living, I thought it was more sacrifice, I thought it was more obedience, I thought it was more righteousness, I thought it was all based on actions and purity. Whether you are on the rock or whether you are on the cross, the only way you are in either place is because of the blood and grace and mercy of Jesus Christ. The difference is living in the promises as a King's child and receiving your inheritance, or living in the sufficiency of a land controlled by a righteous king.

Either you understand the King has given you access to his kingdom's wealth (this doesn't mean earthly wealth necessarily, although it can) or it means that you view yourself as a humble servant never able to enter the kingdom until you die. As a servant, we can trick ourselves into thinking we are humbly serving out of a content and upright heart. When, in reality, we simply don't have the confidence to face the giants that live in our faith.

God's earthly church has allowed people to live defeated lives for too long because we don't have enough leaders who have faced their fears and watched God win their battles. Often, if they have seen God win, then they have kept their voices silent and not passed on the wealth of knowledge that comes from victorious living. Churches have led people to believe that our faith is all about whether we are saved or unsaved. Christ took care of that the moment you trusted the cross. It has everything to do with living a victorious mature Holy Spirit guided liberated life. The church has preached salvation for so long that we don't even know what true kingdom living is. Keep reading and asking the Holy Spirit to reveal the difference.

Learn how to properly identify where you are on the journey, and submit every way of yours to the Holy Sprit's leading of your sixth sense. Remember this final step is further down the cross. Everybody's time on the journey is different. I am just trying to help you identify where you might be at on your personal journey. If I can help you go through the phases more effectively, then praise the Lord.

I grew up in an era where my predecessors believed it was a right of passage for all those who came behind them to struggle with the same pain they did in order to get where they are. I reject that mindset entirely. If you can learn through my pain and ignorance and through my trials and tribulations, then please heed my voice. Let your journey be a fraction of my time.

When you yield and trust in God's promises, much of the pain of these final battles is relieved. (I say much because God has unique ways of helping you to see where your patterns of behavior run deep.)

What if you decide that you do not want to take that final step of trust? Then I am here to tell you that there is happiness and contentment on both sides of this decision. God's grace and provision is never a disappointment; however, there is true fulfillment and incredible living if you take the final step. There is also the knowledge that God wants to use you to help others in a deeper way. You cannot help them reach that final step and experience true victory if you don't take the final step yourself.

It is really your choice. For your emotional well-being, I would not encourage a long stay in this stage of the journey. It will be a painful experience.

If you go back to the wilderness journey of the Israelites in the biblical example, they had their families, they had jobs, they always had everything they needed, but never what they wanted. They learned to accept that way of life. It certainly wasn't what they wanted, but it sure was a lot easier than facing the enemy that lived in their promised land. If you don't finish taking this final step, then what the Israelites experienced is what you will experience. You will experience God's protection and provision, but there will always be the sense of something missing. You will not be living in the abundance of God's blessing. You will not be living in liberty.

When we moved to North Carolina, we lost everything. We literally had to start all over. But as God opened doors, His provision has far exceeded our imagination. He is still in the process of showing us how amazing His provision really is. He keeps allowing us to test His promises, and each time He comes through in more abundance than we could imagine. It has not been in our timing at all. It has been in His timing. It took us nine months before I even had a job that paid the bills. It took Him nine months to provide for my mom financially in ways that far exceeded any capability that I had. It took Him eleven months before I got to see the first wave of people come to Christ. But what I have seen is that He has not failed on his promises yet. What I have discovered is that His promises have nothing to do with my hard work. They have everything to do with my trust in Him.

This is so true of our lives. It is much easier to live with what we know, than to face down the enemy that feels like it could destroy us.

The choice is entirely up to you. I totally get it if you want to just live your life on the grace of Christ and wait for death to bring you the victory of eternal life. If you make that choice, know that the promise of complete surrender is here for you any time you choose, you will just have to let God help you identify what your giants are. If you really want to know, He will show you.

THE "HEBREWS" SENSE - CHPT 8

> ***For you have been called to live in freedom****—not freedom to satisfy your sinful nature, but* ***freedom to serve one another in love. So I advise you to live according to your new life in the Holy Spirit. Then you won't be doing what your sinful nature craves.*** *The old sinful nature loves to do evil, which is just opposite from what the Holy Spirit wants. And the Spirit gives us desires that are opposite from what the sinful nature desires. These two forces are constantly fighting each other, and your choices are never free from this conflict. But when you are directed by the Holy Spirit, you are no longer subject to the law.* Galatians 5:13-18 NLT

This passage in Galatians gives us a view into the freedom and the liberty that I spoke of in the last chapter. **The Holy Spirit has come to deliver us from our sinful desires.** He has come to give us victory over any sin that we struggle with, any fear that we hold onto, any lack of trust that may still exist within us. The Holy Spirit has come to give us liberty and freedom. This chapter is going to reveal what the Holy Spirit is trying to lead us to if we would learn to listen to Him and yield to Him completely. This chapter is where we get to define what God created us for – to be in relationship with Him.

What you read in this chapter is our final goal. It would be awesome if we could actually set this as our final destination in our "sixth Sense" GPS. The passage in Galatians identifies for us that we will always be in conflict within ourselves between wanting to sin and wanting to please God, but when we let the Holy Spirit guide our sixth sense along, we are no longer under the condemnation of the law. That means our last step into complete surrender has nothing to do with us. Instead, it has everything to do with trusting what the Holy Spirit has done in us.

Let me show you a picture of where God desires us to be, to where the cross of Christ can take us even before we get to heaven, and to where the Holy Spirit is trying to guide your sixth sense:

If only we, as a Christian body, would aspire to be here instead of being content with just living on the grace and the cross of Jesus Christ. While it is awesome and mandatory to be dependent upon the grace of Christ, if all we ever do in our churches is tell people this is the best that they can ever experience this side of heaven, we have sold them short of where God has uniquely designed them to be.

Many churches are not capable of leading individuals to this point in their walk because many pastors and teachers don't even believe it is possible to get here before we die.

In the book of Hebrews, the first five chapters help us identify the work of Jesus Christ and properly identify where God wants us to be in our ability to listen to our sixth sense. Take a look at some of these passages from the book of Hebrews:

> *In the past God spoke to our forefathers through the prophets at many times and in various ways, but in these last days he has spoken to us by his Son, whom he appointed heir of all things, and through whom he made the universe. The Son is the radiance of God's glory and the exact representation of his being, sustaining all things by his powerful word. After he had provided purification for sins, he sat down at the right hand of the Majesty in heaven.* Hebrews 1:1-3

God has and is now speaking to us through Christ. He is the only way to get to where God has designed us to be. Christ made the way possible for us through the purification of our sins. If you have not yet put your faith and trust in Jesus Christ, you will never get here. Jesus is the only way to God. Again, the book of Hebrews starts us out by understanding that core truth.

Keep reading what the author of Hebrews states:

> *We must pay more careful attention, therefore, to what we have heard, so that we do not drift away. For if the message spoken by angels was binding, and every violation and disobedience received its just punishment, how shall we escape if we ignore such a great salvation? This salvation, which was first announced by the Lord, was confirmed to us by those who heard him.* Hebrews 2:1-3

We must be careful what we believe about what Christ did. If others didn't escape punishment, then we won't either if we don't stay true to this teaching of salvation. Are we staying true to the teachings in Hebrews?

God confirms in us, through His Holy Spirit guiding our sixth sense, that these teachings are real.

God also testified to it by signs, wonders and various miracles, and gifts of the Holy Spirit distributed according to his will. Hebrews 2:4

How many times have you gotten to the point in your journey where you feel like there is something missing, and you just don't know what it is? This is it. Our western, pragmatic society is so opposed to any type of decision being based upon the power of the Holy Spirit that we have all but eliminated the power He has to guide our sixth sense.

Aren't you glad your finger and your brain cooperated the last time you touched that hot pan? Imagine cutting out one of your other senses. We would have to learn a whole new way of life, and depending upon the sense, we may not even live very long. But the guide that we need to be the most reliant upon in our spiritual journey is the one that many spiritual leaders have removed from our equation. It is time to pay attention to the Holy Spirit.

I have been very intentional to not to use the terms, "baptism of the Holy Spirit," "full gospel," "the filling of the Holy Spirit," "the second work of grace" and so on. I have avoided them on purpose. I think I am coining a new phrase; I want us to be aware of our "Hebrews sense."

Why dub living by the Holy Spirit the "Hebrews Sense?" God created us to be Christ followers as described in the book of Hebrews. The book of Hebrews contains very clear instructions of what a mature follower of Christ should look like. It points to the Holy Spirit's work in a Christ follower's life all throughout. How appropriate that a mature Christ follower's faith is found in the book of Hebrews (the term Hebrew is another name for the Israelites that we have been talking about throughout this book.) They were the ones who experienced the Promised Land living. The Holy Spirit promises to lead us to our Promised Land here on Earth. Christ has certainly set up and established his Heavenly Eternal kingdom. He is coming back to get those who choose to follow Him, but He also came to this earth that we might have access to His kingdom while we are here on earth. We have access to His kingdom right now through the work of the Holy Spirit in our lives.

My friends, many of us cannot ever make it to this point because we are following teachers who have never reached this point themselves. It is a tragedy that has befallen our modern church. We have castrated ourselves from the power of the living God. We have all but removed the power of the Holy Spirit and left God's church, His children, impotent in their spiritual lives.

For those of you who have been a part of our faithful flocks, to all of you who have hungered in your hearts for something more, on behalf of negligent church leaders everywhere, let me say we are sorry. We have failed, and it has had a devastating effect upon many lives. How can we teach people to go to a place where we have never been?

God the Father has been calling us to His rock and all we have done is show them Jesus. That is great, but there is so much more. Jesus said he is going to send someone in his place. Someone that is going to help us do even greater things than Him. We need to help people understand how they can experience the freedom of living in God's kingdom here on earth, while we wait for the return of Christ to take us to our eternal Kingdom.

> [12] *Very truly I tell you, whoever believes in me will do the works I have been doing, and they will do even greater things than these, because I am going to the Father.* [15] *"If you love me, keep my commands.* [16] *And I will ask the Father, and he will give you another advocate to help you and be with you forever—* [17] *the Spirit of truth. The world*

> *cannot accept him, because it neither sees him nor knows him. But you know him, for he lives with you and will be in you.* [23] *Jesus replied, "Anyone who loves me will obey my teaching. My Father will love them, and we will come to them and make our home with them.* [24] *Anyone who does not love me will not obey my teaching. These words you hear are not my own; they belong to the Father who sent me.* [25] *"All this I have spoken while still with you.* [26] *But the Advocate, the Holy Spirit, whom the Father will send in my name, will teach you all things and will remind you of everything I have said to you.* [27] *Peace I leave with you; my peace I give you. I do not give to you as the world gives. Do not let your hearts be troubled and do not be afraid.* [28] *"You heard me say, 'I am going away and I am coming back to you.' If you loved me, you would be glad that I am going to the Father, for the Father is greater than I.* John 14:12-28

The book of Hebrews continues to say that we are delivered from death and the fear of death because of the work of Christ. It says we are delivered from slavery because of the cross of Christ. This slavery is the slavery of trying to measure up to some standard of righteousness that we cannot attain on our own.

> *Since the children have flesh and blood, he too shared in their humanity so that by his death he might destroy him who holds the power of death—*

that is, the devil—and free those who all their lives were held in slavery by their fear of death. Hebrews 2:14-15

See if this picture rings any bells:

Your sixth sense has guided you to the work of Christ on the cross, but it keeps going. The author of Hebrews doesn't stop there, or I should say the Holy Spirit in the book of Hebrews doesn't stop right there.

"So, as the Holy Spirit says: 'Today, if you hear his voice,[8] do not harden your hearts as you did in the rebellion, during the time of testing in the desert, where your fathers tested and tried me and for forty years saw what I did. That is why I was angry with that generation, and I said, 'Their hearts are always going astray, and they have not known my

> *ways.' So I declared on oath in my anger, 'They shall never enter my rest.' See to it, brothers, that none of you has a sinful, unbelieving heart that turns away from the living God. But encourage one another daily, as long as it is called Today, so that none of you may be hardened by sin's deceitfulness. We have come to share in Christ if we hold firmly till the end the confidence we had at first.* Hebrews 3:7-14

How many of us will die in our rebellion? How many of us will die while ignoring the Holy Spirit? How many of us will die in the land of frustration because we fail to take the final step that gets us to the side where God has designed us to be?

Don't give into the lie that says I will never overcome… or the lie that says, this is the best that it will ever get. Don't grieve the Holy Spirit and make Him discipline you because you want to go back from where you came. Let the Holy Spirit guide you to trust God entirely, and to live like heirs of the King while here on earth.

Where do you want to be in this picture?

Your location in this picture is up to you. Just know that you are equipped to be on the far right. I challenge you to make it your desire that anywhere in this picture is not okay unless you are on the far right. If you do not aspire for this or even believe it is possible, then there is a very good chance you will end up either on the far left, or at the very least, you will never truly experience God's rest, God's freedom, God's liberty, and God's kingdom on this side of heaven.

> *"Therefore, since the promise of entering his rest still stands, let us be careful that none of you be found to have fallen short of it. For we also have had the gospel preached to us, just as they did; but the message they heard was of no value to them, because those who heard did not combine it with faith. Now we who have believed enter that rest, just as God has said, So I declared on oath in my anger, 'They shall never enter my rest.' And yet his work has been finished since the creation of the world."* Hebrews 4:1-3

God's rest, this place of true peace and fulfillment, has been prepared since the beginning of time. This final destination is perfectly possible and should be our greatest desire. The destination and the way according to the Bible has been established since the beginning. We get there by faith, and obedience, and trust. Christ made the way possible to this kingdom of promise, and He sent the Holy Spirit to guide us to it, and to help us on our journey as we wait for eternal reward.

> *"It still remains that some will enter that rest, and those who formerly had the gospel preached to them did not go in, because of their disobedience."*
> Hebrews 4:6

Some of you will read this and you will become an obedient, Holy Spirit-led, sixth sense Christ follower. Some of you are going to hear it and still live in disobedience to the Holy Spirit. I am sure someone will even create an exegetical study as to why what I am saying is false in order to justify impotent living and "biblical" teachings.

The key to powerful Spirit-led living is in the book of Hebrews. You need to read the whole book to see all that God has provided for us through Christ and the Holy Spirit. If you don't understand something in the book, find someone or a study guide to help you understand the context of the book of Hebrews.

It is very important that you make reading the Bible a part of your daily life. The Bible is the Holy Spirit's word to you. He speaks to us through the Scriptures. It is important to note here that as we read the word of God, you might "sense" the Holy Spirit's leading in your life. Know that He will never go against his Word! You have heard me say that God told me something or spoke to me. In each of those occasions, it was through the Word. He has never told me to do anything that would be extra-biblical or against the scriptures. If you don't read the Word, then you won't know these things.

There is a very good reason why we can learn to trust and be guided by our sixth sense when we learn that the Holy Spirit will not go against His word. The reason can be found in the book of Hebrews:

> *For the word of God is living and active. Sharper than any double-edged sword, it penetrates even to dividing soul and spirit, joints and marrow; it judges the thoughts and attitudes of the heart. Nothing in all creation is hidden from God's sight. Everything is uncovered and laid bare before the eyes of him to*

whom we must give account. Hebrews 4:12-13

How is God capable of judging the thoughts and attitudes of the heart? How is everything laid bare before his eyes? How did he know that me breaking my leg would yield repentance? How did he know having a near-death experience would shape my trust in Him? How did he know telling us to move to North Carolina would yield the completion of this book? How does He know how to interact with every single human being on the face of this earth in a unique and special way? It is by the Holy Spirit. The Spirit is the one that is capable of interacting with our spirit.

You must make a decision about what you believe, letting the Holy Spirit guide you. Don't sell yourself short because it goes against what you have been taught, or you if don't know if you agree yet. Keep reading and test what the Word of God is saying. Trusting the word of God is the biggest step in reaching the other side.

It is perfectly possible to relate with God, to hear from God, and to enter into His rest. His rest is your promised land. It is that place where you have perfect peace. It is that place where you have perfect trust in Him. It is that place where in the midst of uncertainty, there is complete clarity. It is that place of complete surrender to His will. It is that place of utter dependence upon Him. It is that place where we experience His strength and victory over sin, not our personal will power and self-discipline. It is that place where you are less and He is more. It is that place where you are doing everything that you can do while realizing that life has nothing to do with you. His rest, His kingdom, is accessible to us here on this earth. To experience this rest is the very reason that Christ paid the price He did. Realize that this is the final destination that the Holy Spirit is trying to guide you to.

THE REALITY - CHPT 9

We have four chapters left in our journey of learning to live by the guidance of the Holy Spirit, and unfortunately I realize the reality that is about to happen.

You started this book at some point of reference and you will end this book at some point of reference in this picture:

Again, the Scriptures through the power of the Holy Spirit have prepared us for the reality of life. Let's look at the reality that many of us desire not to deal with:

> *Jesus answered: "Watch out that no one deceives you. For many will come in my name, claiming, 'I am the Christ,' and will deceive many. You will hear*

> *of wars and rumors of wars, but see to it that you are not alarmed. Such things must happen, but the end is still to come. Nation will rise against nation, and kingdom against kingdom. There will be famines and earthquakes in various places. All these are the beginning of birth pains. 'Then you will be handed over to be persecuted and put to death, and you will be hated by all nations because of me. At that time many will turn away from the faith and will betray and hate each other, and many false prophets will appear and deceive many people. Because of the increase of wickedness, the love of most will grow cold, but he who stands firm to the end will be saved.'"* Matthew 24:4-13

Jesus Himself prepares us for the reality of what is going to happen. There are going to be many teachers that come saying they are teaching the way to god. Christ in this passage is the one who points the way to God. Most religions have some prophet or many prophets that declare the way to god or the higher power. Jesus warns us that there are going to be many that are going to make really good arguments that their way is the right way. They are going to deceive many people. He warns us that our sixth sense is going to be easily deceived.

He then warns us that there will be horrible things that happen to those who continue to believe that he is the only way across that divide. He warns us that those that call upon Him will be hated and ridiculed, and He warns us that many of us will not be able to handle the pressure.

Because of the teachings of Jesus in this passage, it is important that we realize that when we enter God's rest, it does not always mean our circumstances will be what we want them to be. Prosperity and earthly peace may be a part of your personal experience, but that is part of your story. Be grateful if that is your story. God's rest is an internal peace amid our circumstances. It is an internal rest that says, "I know I am right where God wants me to be. I am at peace and I am going to trust God's promises because I have followed and listened to the Holy Spirit all along my journey."

Jesus is warning us that regardless of circumstances, we must stand firm in Him until the very end. He is warning us that we must continue to listen to the Holy Spirit to discern what is true and what is false. He is warning us not to be deceived by those who preach something contrary to Him. We must be able to identify if someone is a false prophet, and we must stand firm against the deception of sin. The Holy Spirit helps us do this through the Word of God. "If" we do all that, then "he who stands firm until the end will be saved."

When is the end? The end is either when you die or when Jesus returns. But even Jesus tells us that the reality we have to deal with is that many people are going to be deceived by false teachings and sin. There are roughly 7 billion people in this world right now, and roughly a third of them believe in Jesus. Many are being deceived. That is why we must choose to be Hebrew Christ followers. If you choose to be a Hebrew Christ follower, I can assure you, you will be one of those who stands firm. You will see how it works in the next chapter.

Look at what else the Bible says: Remember that the Holy Spirit wrote the Bible, and the Holy Spirit will not contradict Himself. If you are ever tempted to think that some sin is okay in your life, then the Holy Spirit is not guiding you.

> *Not everyone who says to me, 'Lord, Lord,' will enter the kingdom of heaven, but only he who does the will of my Father who is in heaven. Many will say to me on that day, 'Lord, Lord, did we not prophesy in your name, and in your name drive out demons and perform many miracles?' Then I will tell them plainly, 'I never knew you. Away from me, you evildoers!' "Therefore everyone who hears these words of mine and puts them into practice is like a wise man who built his house on the rock. The rain came down, the streams rose, and the winds*

> *blew and beat against that house; yet it did not fall, because it had its foundation on the rock.* Matthew 7:21-25

Again, Jesus is giving us the reality. Many people will think they are okay simply because they have cried out "Lord, Lord." Simply because they have seen God do amazing things. However, because of the rains and the storms of life, because people will give up in the difficult times of life, because people fail to listen to the Holy Spirit guide them through these difficult and tumultuous times they will not be known by God, they will not be saved. Remember the picture of the little guy standing with one foot on the cross and one foot on land. These "storms" keep us from truly trusting Christ and this breaks my heart.

Jesus warns us yet again about the reality of what we are up against in another passage of Scripture:

> *Listen then to what the parable of the sower means: When anyone hears the message about the kingdom and does not understand it, the evil one comes and snatches away what was sown in his heart. This is the seed sown along the path. The one who received the seed that fell on rocky places is the man who hears the word and at once receives it with joy. But since he has no root, he lasts only a*

short time. When trouble or persecution comes because of the word, he quickly falls away. The one who received the seed that fell among the thorns is the man who hears the word, but the worries of this life and the deceitfulness of wealth choke it, making it unfruitful. But the one who received the seed that fell on good soil is the man who hears the word and understands it. He produces a crop, yielding a hundred, sixty or thirty times what was sown. Matthew 13:18-23

According to Jesus there will be those who hear the Word of God, they will respond to their sixth sense, and start their own journey. Then, because they fail to listen to the Holy Spirit in the difficult times, they are going to turn away. Again, this passage is like the person who stands on left side of the cross, they may even put a foot on the cross but they never truly sell out. They test the waters and then decide to turn back.

Jesus is warning us that because of the work of the Holy Spirit there will be troubles and persecution. Jesus tells us that the Word is going to seem contrary to their personal worries. This teaching identifies why it is so hard to trust God. The worries of this life will choke some out. The deceitfulness of wealth is going to lead some astray. Some are going to put one foot on the cross, they hear the Holy

Spirit calling, take that first step and soon realize what they have gotten themselves into. According to the scripture they are then going to turn and walk right back to where they came from. Their faith will not take root.

While I realize this is the reality, I also realize that there are many who really want to believe in Jesus. I know it is not easy holding on to the Christian faith. Anyone that thinks Christianity is a crutch is clearly not a Christian. Many are going to deny and reject what Christ has made possible through the Holy Spirit. I realize this, and I battle. I battle for you. I battle for all who are lost. I don't want anyone to turn back. I don't want anyone to fall short. I don't want anyone to give up because "it seems too hard."

Knowing what the reality would look like, see what Jesus says He is going to do. Please hear the words of Jesus. They are so important to us.

> *Then he opened their minds so they could understand the Scriptures. He told them, 'This is what is written: The Christ will suffer and rise from the dead on the third day, and repentance and forgiveness of sins will be preached in his name to all nations, beginning at Jerusalem. You are witnesses of these things. I am going to send you what my Father has promised; but stay in the city*

until you have been clothed with power from on high. Luke 24:45-49

Jesus told the disciples this after He opened their minds to understand the Scriptures, the Word. He says, "Hey guys, I am going away, and in my place I am going to send you another power. In fact, this other power is so important don't do anything, don't go anywhere until you get it."

What power was He sending them? Christ was sending them the power of the Holy Spirit! The very thing He said not to leave the city without is the very thing that many churches, denominations, and teachers preach, teach, and live without: the power of the Holy Spirit.

When you live like a Hebrews Christ follower, when you live how this book is challenging you to live, when you get to the next chapter and you actually embrace what is being taught, you will have a power from on high that you cannot imagine, but it will come at the cost of all that we have talked about thus far. Jesus explains it further in the book of John:

"If you love me, you will obey what I command. And I will ask the Father, and he will give you another Counselor to be with you forever-- the Spirit of truth. The world cannot accept him, because it

> *neither sees him nor knows him. But you know him, for he lives with you and will be in you. I will not leave you as orphans; I will come to you. Before long, the world will not see me anymore, but you will see me. Because I live, you also will live. On that day you will realize that I am in my Father, and you are in me, and I am in you. Whoever has my commands and obeys them, he is the one who loves me. He who loves me will be loved by my Father, and I too will love him and show myself to him."*
> John 14:15-21

If we love Jesus, we will obey Him! He gives us the ability to obey by sending us the Holy Spirit. Where do we find how to obey him? The instructions are in the Word of God. Jesus is telling His disciples, "I am going away, but I am sending you another person, a counselor." Why do we need a counselor? We need a counselor because life is going to get bumpy. Christ is sending us what we need. We don't need more psychologists, psychiatrists, drugs and anxiety pills. We need the church to start teaching the truth and dependence upon the Holy Spirit. (Please don't let your mind go down the road of whether or not psychologists, psychiatrists, and medications are bad. That is not my point, but I know some will get hung up on that.)

The Holy Spirit will guide you as you determine what you believe. Don't ask your neighbor about this; no one has ever seen the Holy Spirit. You can't see the Holy Spirit, but you know He is there. Jesus promises, "I am not going to leave you alone. I may be gone, but I am sending you someone even better. I am sending you the one who will be with you always." Verse 20 clearly identifies this process. He also clearly identifies that access to the Holy Spirit is granted through obedient behavior, and submission to the Word of God.

Disobedient behavior, lack of submission, lack of trust, and lack of surrender are a great portion of our problem! Human nature doesn't like to submit to anything. Jesus calls himself Lord. I don't know if you realize this, but when someone is Lord over you, you submit to everything they say or they are not Lord. Too many people want to walk the bridge of Christ without making Him Lord of their lives.

Jesus doesn't stop telling us about the Holy Spirit either. He continues with the following:

> *Then Judas (not Judas Iscariot) said," But, Lord, why do you intend to show yourself to us and not to the world?" Jesus replied," If anyone loves me, he will obey my teaching. My Father will love him, and we*

> *will come to him and make our home with him. He who does not love me will not obey my teaching. These words you hear are not my own; they belong to the Father who sent me. All this I have spoken while still with you. But the Counselor, the Holy Spirit, whom the Father will send in my name, will teach you all things and will remind you of everything I have said to you. Peace I leave with you; my peace I give you. I do not give to you as the world gives. Do not let your hearts be troubled and do not be afraid."* John 14:22-27

Again, Jesus clarifies our journey towards Him is done in obedience. In order to aid us on that journey of following Him, He is sending us the Counselor, the Holy Spirit, who is going to guide us and instruct us in all truth. Jesus is promising us this Holy Spirit. After Jesus left the earth and ascended to heaven, the New Testament centers around the teaching of the Holy Spirit. The rest of the New Testament is given because of the Holy Spirit's work in people's lives.

This passage in John also gives us a clear picture of the "rest" that God promises in the book of Hebrews. Jesus calls it "peace." He is going to leave us access to the very peace He had access to: He is giving us peace in the midst of uncertainty and trying times. If anybody's life reflects peace in the midst of difficulty, it would be Jesus'. He sent us the

Holy Spirit so we can have the same peace. This peace is learned as we journey across the cross of Christ learning to hear and respond and trust the Holy Spirit as the guide of our sixth sense.

Look at what happened after Jesus was crucified:

> *"After his suffering, he showed himself to these men and gave many convincing proofs that he was alive. He appeared to them over a period of forty days and spoke about the kingdom of God. On one occasion, while he was eating with them, he gave them this command: "Do not leave Jerusalem, but wait for the gift my Father promised, which you have heard me speak about. For John baptized with water, but in a few days you will be baptized with the Holy Spirit." So, when they met together, they asked him, "Lord, are you at this time going to restore the kingdom to Israel?" He said to them:" It is not for you to know the times or dates the Father has set by his own authority. But you will receive power when the Holy Spirit comes on you; and you will be my witnesses in Jerusalem, and in all Judea and Samaria, and to the ends of the earth."* Acts 1:3-8

Jesus sent the Holy Spirit to give us power in this life to overcome the difficulties that we will all face. Because all of us have our own unique difficulties, Christ gives us the Holy

Spirit to guide each of us on our unique journey. Think about it. What a person deals with in their faith as their struggle in America is far different than a person who has chosen to follow Christ growing up in North Korea. Yet the power of the Holy Spirit is here to guide each of us in a unique way. The Spirit is here to counsel us in what we need to hold on to the truth no matter our unique circumstances. The Holy Spirit is a power that is not of ourselves and cannot be seen, but it is a power that enables us to be obedient witnesses for Him. Christ gives us the power of the Holy Spirit so that in our circumstances, we will have all that is necessary so that we can point others to the glory of God. It is like we each have our own personal GPS and power source for the life that we each have. What a promise of good news that is!

Unfortunately, some Christians are living without this power that Christ promised to send simply because we don't regularly teach it and we seldom help people learn to understand it.

It is a very good thing that the early disciples didn't disobey Christ when He said, "don't go anywhere until you get this power that I am speaking of." We ignore this "power" all the time in our churches (especially the western church), and then we wonder why nothing is happening.

Look at what the disciples experienced while living in obedience waiting for the promised, powerful Holy Spirit!

> *When the day of Pentecost came, they were all together in one place. Suddenly a sound like the blowing of a violent wind came from heaven and filled the whole house where they were sitting. They saw what seemed to be tongues of fire that separated and came to rest on each of them. All of them were filled with the Holy Spirit and began to speak in other tongues as the Spirit enabled them. Now there were staying in Jerusalem God-fearing Jews from every nation under heaven. When they heard this sound, a crowd came together in bewilderment, because each one heard them speaking in his own language. Utterly amazed, they asked:" Are not all these men who are speaking Galileans? Then how is it that each of us hears them in his own native language? Parthians, Medes and Elamites; residents of Mesopotamia, Judea and Cappadocia, Pontus and Asia, Phrygia and Pamphylia, Egypt and the parts of Libya near Cyrene; visitors from Rome (both Jews and converts to Judaism); Cretans and Arabs--we hear them declaring the wonders of God in our own tongues!' Amazed and perplexed, they asked one another, 'What does this mean?' Some, however, made fun of them and said, 'They have had too much wine.' Then Peter stood up with the Eleven, raised his voice and addressed the crowd: 'Fellow Jews and all*

of you who live in Jerusalem, let me explain this to you; listen carefully to what I say. These men are not drunk, as you suppose. It's only nine in the morning! No, this is what was spoken by the prophet Joel; "In the last days, God says, I will pour out my Spirit on all people. Your sons and daughters will prophesy, your young men will see visions, your old men will dream dreams. Even on my servants, both men and women, I will pour out my Spirit in those days, and they will prophesy. I will show wonders in the heaven above and signs on the earth below, blood and fire and billows of smoke. The sun will be turned to darkness and the moon to blood before the coming of the great and glorious day of the Lord. And everyone who calls on the name of the Lord will be saved." Acts 2:1-21

I know that is a long passage to read, but in it lies a power from on high. Don't freak out. I am not going to tell you that you have to speak in tongues to receive power.

What I am saying is, when you learn to live with the Holy Spirit guiding your sixth sense, you will receive power! You will receive a power that will be difficult to explain. Some will laugh at you and mock you and ridicule you. Some will doubt you, and you will definitely be misunderstood. Still others will wonder and be attracted to what you have to say and ultimately many will come to the saving knowledge of

Jesus Christ because of you allowing the Holy Spirit to work through your life. Christ has sent this power not for us to look good in this world, but that we would be equipped with whatever we need to be able to point others to the glory of God. The power of the Holy Spirit is going to look different in each one of our lives, but it will always point others to God.

This is what Christ paid the ultimate price for each of us to experience. **Because we can't wrap up this teaching and say exactly how it is going to look in each person's life, churches all across the world live without this power.** Many churches avoid talking about it simply because it is so difficult to explain. Because we cannot see, taste, touch, or smell the power of the Holy Spirit, some say that it is not real. Still others ignore it because it cannot be explained. Yet we are all aware there is a supernatural power around us. Because it is a difficult yet simple concept to wrap our minds around, we choose to live impotent spiritual lives.

I want all of us to live in the power of Jesus Christ and the Holy Spirit. Keep reading and let the Holy Spirit guide your sixth sense to make a decision about the truth.

THE SPIRITUAL KINGDOM - CHPT 10

How I long for God's church to live in the truth of the book of Hebrews and to be Hebrews Christ followers.

> *Therefore let us leave the elementary teachings about Christ and go on to maturity, not laying again the foundation of repentance from acts that lead to death, and of faith in God, instruction about baptisms, the laying on of hands, the resurrection of the dead, and eternal judgment. And God permitting, we will do so.* Hebrews 6:1-3

I pray that you are ready to move on to the maturity that the Holy Spirit is calling us to. This final step of maturity is a crucial step. Remember when I shared with you about the discipline that the Holy Spirit has to take us through? This final step comes with great responsibility. The Holy Spirit helps us take this final step when He knows we are ready for it. I personally believe all of us are created with the ability to take this step. I pray that you are willing to do so.

> *It is impossible for those who have once been enlightened, who have tasted the heavenly gift, who have shared in the Holy Spirit, who have tasted the goodness of the word of God and the powers of the coming age, if they fall away, to be brought back to repentance, because to their loss they are crucifying the Son of God all over again and*

subjecting him to public disgrace. Hebrews 6:4-6

This passage says it is impossible for those of us who have been enlightened, for those who have walked across the cross of Christ and been filled with the Holy Spirit, for those who have experienced how good the Word of God is, who have experienced the truth of the Holy Spirit, for those who have entered His rest… *it is* impossible for those who have experienced the Holy Spirit's power to be brought back to repentance if they fall away. What does that mean?

Let me show you the picture then we can talk about the answer.

Remember how Christ said He wants us to be on solid ground for when the storms and the trials of life come upon us? He promised us we would have trouble in this life. This is how He wants us to stand firm amidst those trials. This is it. This is where He wants us. Remember when He said,

"The Father and I are one, I and the Spirit are one and you and I are one." This is how that picture comes to completion. Many Christians believe that this final picture is only for heaven. This is the spiritual kingdom that Christ came to bring us while we are waiting for our eternity in heaven. This is our heaven on earth, our promised land when we learn to live as mature, obedient, Holy Spirit-led Hebrews Christ followers.

Do you see in the picture why it is so crucial that the Holy Spirit knows he has our complete surrender before he nudges us to this point? What is missing?

The bridge is missing. This passage in Hebrews makes it clear if we get here we cannot go back. It is impossible either because no sane person would want to go back where they came from, you can't do it because God said it is impossible, or the cross is gone because the Scriptures said we cannot crucify Christ twice. Any way you want to interpret the passage, the picture remains the same. The bridge is gone, and death alone awaits us if we try to return to the world's ways. (Personally I believe that it would be impossible to go back. Once you get to this point in life you can't go back, it is spiritually impossible.)

Please understand the picture is symbolic of your journey. The Cross of Christ is never gone. At this stage, it is utter foolishness to go backwards. If you try going backwards at this point it will yield fruitless despondency in your spiritual life. It will yield a personal internal death. Christ came that we might have life to the full. All throughout the scriptures whenever God's people "turned back" it never worked out.

If there is so much responsibility with this final step, you might wonder why anyone would want to take this final step? The biggest reason is that we should want to be mature Christ followers so that we can point others to God as well. We should want to experience the fullness of the word of God. We should want to experience the power of the Holy Spirit. We should want to experience the promised land for the believer. We should want to experience His rest!

The Jewish people are still waiting for their Messiah to establish an earthly kingdom of peace and prosperity, but Jesus the Messiah said He already brought His kingdom with Him. He brought His spiritual kingdom, which exists in having a right relationship with God. He will bring His physical kingdom with Him the second time around. He left us with an amazing kingdom to live in while He was gone. Yet most Christ followers never enter it because they are told it can't be entered, because they don't want to enter it until they die, or because they don't know that it is even possible to enter it. What a tragedy!

Being a Holy Spirit-led, mature Hebrews Christ follower is that spiritual kingdom—the kingdom where we learn to rely upon the Holy Spirit for our daily power; where God has complete access to every area of our lives, where we live in obedience to the Word of God. Does that mean we will never sin? By no means! It means we desire not to sin.

The key to this spiritual kingdom is not the absence of sin. It is not some amazing ability to be able to adhere to an incredible list of righteous behavior and legalistic rules. It is a condition of the heart and desires. It is the difference between youthfulness and adulthood. It is maturity.

Christians are so focused on what to do with sin; Christ followers are focused on what to do with life. Christians are focused upon the religiosity of faith; Christ followers are focused upon the life that Christ came to bring to all people. Jesus didn't come to condemn us. He came to pave the way to life—life that is more abundant. Life that is full. Life that is capable of being immeasurably more than we can think or imagine. He came to bring us life free from the anxieties and the worries of the world. He came to deliver us from the power and deception of sin. He came to show us that there is great power when we learn to defeat sin in our lives.

Even though Christ came to bring us a victorious life, most Christ followers' lives are weighed down by the very things we tell others that Jesus came to save them from. What a mixed message we are sending to the world. Do we really have to wonder why more people don't want what we have?

What is the power of sin? It is the deception that sinning would be more fun or fulfilling than living in obedience to the Word of God.

I once had a person ask me, "What do you do when you just really want to be bad, when you just really want to sin?" I didn't know how to answer because the question was very sincere. I didn't want to sound super spiritual, but my answer came and it was very genuine. I simply said, "I really don't want to sin." When we get to this point in our life with Christ and the Holy Spirit we don't want to sin, we want to live. Unfortunately, I still sin, and sometimes I even sin on purpose. But I don't like it. Sin is not as pleasurable. I don't want to sound pious, but at this point in your walk with God, when you sin, it breaks your heart! When you sin, you are saddened by your continued human condition. We are not absent from sin in our lives, but we are genuinely broken by the sin in our lives. There is a key difference. When we sin we quickly right our thinking or behavior and focus on life versus shame, guilt, and anxiety.

Let me give you an example. When I was eleven years old, I saw my first pornographic magazine at Boy Scouts. It opened a struggle that proved to become a severe problem in my life. At age twenty-one, a revival went through the college I was attending (Northwestern Christian University) and God began a process of breaking my addiction, (my problem, many don't believe it can be an addiction.) If you know anything about an addiction/bad habit, the person is consumed with a physiological response that brings fulfillment to them through whatever they are addicted to. It took me years to fully understand my struggle.

Even in my struggle, pleasure was very fleeting. My life was consumed with far more guilt, shame, and defeat than pleasure. The Holy Spirit has taught me how to gain control of the temptations in life and how to have victory versus defeat. The Holy Spirit has taught me how to experience peace and joy and forgiveness, instead of self-hatred, anxiety, shame and guilt. The temptations in life are still all around me, but my focus is different. If the temptations become too strong in my life, then I know my focus is off. How do I know? The Holy Spirit is walking with me and guiding me. He has complete access to my spirit and my mind and my inmost desires.

So, am I saying that when we get here, that everything is hunky dory? By no means! We will have troubles, we will have trials, and we will suffer the storms and the rains of life. But when we are standing on this side of the cross, it doesn't matter what comes our way, we have an incredible peace and knowledge that we know we will make it. We will have life and abundant joy because we will have the power of the Holy Spirit guiding and directing our every step. We will have the Holy Spirit speaking to our sixth sense, leading us into all truth and knowledge of the Word of God. We will have the Holy Spirit opening our eyes to the living, breathing, active Word of God.

When you reach this step in your journey, you will experience God in a whole new way. There is no way to explain this last step until you take it. It is the most amazing place to be. I could not tell you about it if I was not here. There are many who call upon the name of Christ and are empowered by the Holy Spirit, but there is not a lot of information explaining how to get here.

If you want what I am speaking of, then you must be willing to go through steps to maturity. You have to go through each stage of the cross. I said my journey took 40 years to fully understand this process. I lied it has now taken me 43 years. Three more years have passed since I edited this book. Your journey might only take 2 years, or maybe it will take 80 years. I firmly believe it is a continued journey. It is called a journey for a reason, but your journey is heavily impacted by your decisions. There is no magic pill, and I can assure you that you will never reach this point if you don't think it even exists. Living in the peace of God is a beautiful thing. I want you to be able to stand here as well.

When you learn to walk in total surrender to the will of God, which can be found in the Word of God, then you can experience this spiritual kingdom. When you accept that following the way of Christ and all that He did and taught us to do, and when you accept that you have access to His heavenly kingdom here on Earth through the Holy Spirit, then you can experience what I am talking about. When you accept that there should be a power that sets you apart from the rest of mankind, then you can experience the power of the Holy Spirit!

Christ died to give His followers a power from on high to help them save the masses from the throes of death. His cross in my life has led me to a place where His power has come alive in me—and I want everyone to experience it. I don't care what denomination you are from or whether you are a charismatic or a fundamentalist, whether you believe in predestination or free-will, or whether you are Orthodox, Protestant, or Catholic. Christ's cross has the power to lead all who call upon His name to His spiritual kingdom. We get so wrapped up in doctrine that we have lost the power of Christ's kingdom.

If we are ever going to get Christ's power back, then we better start learning to live by the power of the Holy Spirit guiding and directing our sixth sense.

If you are waiting for me to give you a six-point process to get to where I am talking about you have totally missed what has been said. I have been very deliberate in my words. I have purposely avoided many terms typical of "Christian doctrine." I have called this process a journey, and we all must face this journey differently. There are elements that will be similar in all our stories, such as complete surrender, total trust, obedience, submission, changed desires, victory, abundant life, the Word of God, and peace. These are all key elements in the journey, and the final result will be that you will experience a power that points all the attention and glory back to God.

If you want what this book speaks of, look at what Jesus promises you.:

> *Ask and it will be given to you; seek and you will find; knock and the door will be opened to you. For everyone who asks receives; he who seeks finds; and to him who knocks, the door will be opened.* Matthew 7:7-8

If you want what I speak of, seek it out, ask God for it. He will give it to you.

He paved the way directly to the truth, yet we consume our time looking everywhere but the Word of God. Your answers, your hope, your truth, your way, are written and revealed in Scripture. Jesus promises it.

I encourage you to read the rest of the passage in Matthew 7 and see if it does not confirm all that we have talked about thus far. Here is another passage of Scripture in the meantime:

> *So I say to you: Ask and it will be given to you; seek and you will find; knock and the door will be opened to you. For everyone who asks receives; he who seeks finds; and to him who knocks, the door will be opened. "Which of you fathers, if your son asks for a fish, will give him a snake instead? Or if he asks for an egg, will give him a scorpion? If you then, though you are evil, know how to give good gifts to your children, how much more will your Father in heaven give the Holy Spirit to those who ask him!"* Luke 11:9-13

Do you see it there? So many people want to use Christ as their ticket to prosperity. They want Him to give them whatever they ask for, but did you see what Jesus is talking about when He says He will give us what we ask for? He is not talking about healing, or a personal jet, or a money tree. He says if you really want it, seek it. If you really want it, ask for it. If you really want it, knock on the doors of heaven and He will give it to you. What will He give you? He will give you the Holy Spirit. He gave His life that we might have access to the power of the Holy Spirit. Do you want it? Do you *really* want it?

I long for God's children to want what Christ has really come to bring instead of what their hearts desire. Oh, that we would desire what God desires for us.

Let me give you an example. Many Christians fill their prayers with requests for healing from sickness and disease, financial bailouts, relational remedies and freedom from the storms and pressures of life.

The kind of prayers that we need to be praying should embrace the pain and suffering in life. What if it is the pain and suffering in life that God uses in order for us to learn all that He has for us? What if we pray for Him to take away the very suffering that is going to lead us to a proper understanding of our sixth sense? Our human idea of suffering is so contrary to God's Word that our belief system has again left us impotent.

My dad died when I was 14 after more than a four-year battle with cancer. I had one Holy Spirit-teaching person tell me that if my dad would have had more faith, he would have been healed. Really?

Maybe if Jesus would have had more faith, He would have realized that He could have created an easier way to get people to heaven than having to go through the pain of the cross. Maybe Jesus should have had more faith instead of telling us that we would have troubles in this world. Maybe Jesus should have had more faith when He said we will experience trouble because of the Word. I hope you sense my sarcasm.

If you want the power of the Holy Spirit, then you are going to have to give up on the idea that as a Christ Follower, you will escape from the suffering of life. You need to realize that sometimes God must use, and even implement, the suffering times of life to get us to the point where he wants us to be.

Again, Hebrews says,

> *During the days of Jesus' life on earth, he offered up prayers and petitions with loud cries and tears to the one who could save him from death, and he was heard because of his reverent submission. Although he was a son, he learned obedience from what he suffered and, once made perfect, he became the source of eternal salvation for all who obey him.* Hebrews 5:7-9

If you want the Holy Spirit to guide your sixth sense to truth, the answer lies in the book of Hebrews. We are called to be mature, Hebrew Christ followers, but we are so desperate for some easy pill for God to take away the pain. We are so desperate for God to take things away that we fail to see what God wants to guide us through.

When you are a Hebrews-empowered, Holy Spirit-led Christ follower, your perspective on all that you are and all that you go through in life will change.

Again, it is all about the journey. Where do you want to be on your journey? Hebrews points out where many of us are:

> *We have much to say about this, but it is hard to explain because* ***you are slow to learn.*** *In fact, though by this time you ought to be teachers, you need someone to teach you the elementary truths of God's word all over again. You need milk, not solid food! Anyone who lives on milk, being still an infant, is not acquainted with the teaching about righteousness. But solid food is for the mature, who by constant use have trained themselves to distinguish good from evil.* Hebrews 5:11-14

The Holy Spirit has so much more to teach us, but we are so slow to learn. Many of us should be teachers by now, but according to the scriptures we want to suckle from mommy's breast. We want to be coddled and cared for. We want our hands held. We don't want to have to be mature. Please give yourselves over wholly to being a mature Hebrews Christ follower.

Mature, Hebrews, sixth sense, Christ followers can distinguish good from evil because they have been trained all along their journey. For example, even Jesus had to start his ministry by going out into the wilderness of salvation. After God the Father sent the Holy Spirit on him like a dove, He had to be tested for 40 days and nights while fasting. While He was out there, Satan came and tempted Him with horrible, rotten sins, right? No! Satan tested His knowledge of the Word of God. Being a Holy Spirit-led Christ follower is all about being able to properly understand the Word of God, even when Satan tries to twist it in our minds. Are we guided by the Holy Spirit enough that we can identify when Satan is tempting us not just with sin, but when He tempts us with Scripture?

Most of us struggle with identifying how to control a dirty thought or not eat too many cookies, let alone be able to fight off the enemy when he throws Scripture at us.

We have nursed the church along for so long that we have deluded ourselves into thinking that there is no hope until we die and get out of this place. If that is what you think, then you have given into the darkness of your own mind as well.

Death for the Christ follower is certainly the final victory, but according to the Scripture, Christ beat Satan on the cross. When Christ rose from the dead, He dethroned Satan and took away any power that he had, yet the church lives like Satan is still in charge of the world.

Jesus says the gates of hell shall not prevail. Do you really live like you believe that?

YEAH, BUT! YEAH, BUT! - CHPT 11

If you have been raised in the church, you may be thinking, "Yeah, but what are you saying about the gifts of the Spirit and speaking in tongues?"

Let's check the Scriptures and let the Holy Spirit guide your sixth sense.

> *The body is a unit, though it is made up of many parts; and though all its parts are many, they form one body. So it is with Christ. For we were all baptized by one Spirit into one body--whether Jews or Greeks, slave or free--and we were all given the one Spirit to drink. Now the body is not made up of one part but of many. If the foot should say, 'Because I am not a hand, I do not belong to the body,' it would not for that reason cease to be part of the body. so that there should be no division in the body, but that its parts should have equal concern for each other. If one part suffers, every part suffers with it; if one part is honored, every part rejoices with it. Now you are the body of Christ, and each one of you is a part of it. And in the church God has appointed first of all apostles, second prophets, third teachers, then workers of miracles, also those having gifts of healing, those able to help others, those with gifts of administration, and those speaking in different kinds of tongues. Are all apostles? Are all*

> *prophets? Are all teachers? Do all work miracles? Do all have gifts of healing? Do all speak in tongues? Do all interpret? But eagerly desire the greater gifts. And now I will show you the most excellent way.* 1 Corinthians 12:12-15, 25-31

As we see in this passage, there are several different gifts of the Sprit. It is impossible for one person to have all the gifts—we all have different gifts. Just as each of us is at a different point in our journey, we all have different gifts. If God gave one person all the gifts, then there would be no reason for us to learn how to get along in the spirit of love. There is only one body and only one spirit and we must all learn how to get along while each of us evidences the working of the spirit in our lives in a different way.

This book is not about the gifts, but the fact that when you reach the stage of the journey I am talking about, your gift will come alive in you in a new way. You will have new found power that will enable you to exercise your unique spiritual gift mix. If you are a teacher, you will find a new power in all your teaching. If you are a leader (administrator), you will find a new power in the way that you lead. If you heal others, you will have a new power to help heal others. (I would even say this is how many doctors have found cures to rare diseases. There was once a time when Christians led the way in the medical and scientific world. Oh, to have the day again when our doctors and scientists were empowered by the Holy Spirit, instead of the enlightenment.)

Whatever your spiritual gift or gifts may be, and I personally believe all the gifts are alive, if you become a Hebrews follower then you will experience newfound power in your unique gift. The end result will be that your gift will help you lead others to the cross of Christ, the freedom He provides, and the glory of God!

If you want to discover your unique gift mix, there are all kinds of Spiritual Gift Assessments that you can take online or through your local church. Becoming a mature, Hebrews Christ follower will bring your gift to life and attract others to

Christ. We are on earth not to bring glory to ourselves, but to God. The best way to do that is through the power of the Holy Spirit. As a Christ follower, our real home is in another place. God has allowed us the opportunity to convince others that where we are going is where they need to be too. It is time we start living in a way that compels others to come along.

So if you are trying to use this book as a tool to argue about speaking in tongues, prophecy, healing, teaching, giving or any other gift, then you have missed the whole point of why I avoided the topic. These are the very arguments that are dividing God's church. Are the gifts alive? You better believe it. How are they alive, and how are we to use them? We must properly listen and identify what the Holy Spirit is guiding us to do.

We need to address one possible "yeah, but" conversation: yeah, but what is this book saying about eternal salvation?

Let me use another picture to begin the conversation. Let's properly identify what we are saying when we converse about salvation, eternal security, losing your salvation and backsliding. I feel the church has spent too much time talking about this issue, but I realize that it still is a concern for many. So if your brain is telling you we need to clarify this issue, then let's try to do so in a loving manner.

As you read this book, you are somewhere on this journey. Everyone in the world is somewhere on this journey. Sadly, there are many on this journey that have yet to even hear about Jesus, but that is another dilemma. Since you have this book, you are clearly somewhere on this journey.

As we have already discussed in previous chapters, Christ's cross is really strong. As we have already discussed, Jesus himself said some are going to start this journey and quit. As we have already discussed, some try to say they are Christians simply because they can identify that Jesus died and rose from the dead. Even the demons know that one, but it doesn't mean they are Christ followers.

I will tell you how my beliefs look as they are evidenced in this picture. According to my personal study of the Word of God, as long as we are trusting in the work of Christ on the cross and what He did for us and where He desires us to be, then we are saved. Even if we are being fools and jumping up and down on the grace of Jesus Christ.

> *By the grace God has given me, I laid a foundation as an expert builder, and someone else is building on it. But each one should be careful how he builds. For no one can lay any foundation other than the one already laid, which is Jesus Christ. If any man builds on this foundation using gold, silver, costly stones, wood, hay or straw, his work will be shown for what it is, because the Day will bring it to light. It will be revealed with fire, and the fire will test the quality of each man's work. If what he has built survives, he will receive his reward. If it is burned up, he will suffer loss; he himself will be saved, but only as one escaping through the flames. Don't you know that you yourselves are God's temple and that God's Spirit lives in you? If anyone destroys God's temple, God will destroy him; for God's temple is sacred, and you are that temple.* 1 Corinthians 3:10-17

It is a bad idea to take advantage of the grace of Jesus Christ! Even here in Corinthians it says that if you build foolishly upon the foundations of the cross of Christ, you may not have anything to show for it. You may not even make it very long in this world. God may have to destroy you because you are destroying His temple. Why would He care if you are destroying the temple? Your temple, your body, is where the Holy Spirit resides. God makes it a serious business when we start talking about the Holy Spirit. Even if He should bring us into His presence early by destroying us, the Word of God goes on to say that although you may be destroyed, you will make it as though one escaping through the flames.

According to my study of the Word of God, you are saved as long as you are consciously depending upon the cross of Christ and are trying to build upon it. Even this fool mentioned in Corinthians was trying to build upon the cross. His doctrine and His actions in life were unhealthy, but he was saved because his foundation was Jesus Christ!

So am I saying that all someone has to do is trust upon the name of Jesus Christ and they will be saved? Yes.

Look again at Hebrews:

Therefore, since we have a great high priest who has gone through the heavens, Jesus the Son of God, let us hold firmly to the faith we profess. For we do not have a high priest who is unable to sympathize with our weaknesses, but we have one who has been tempted in every way, just as we are--yet was without sin. Let us then approach the throne of grace with confidence, so that we may receive mercy and find grace to help us in our time of need. Every high priest is selected from among men and is appointed to represent them in matters related to God, to offer gifts and sacrifices for sins. He is able to deal gently with those who are ignorant and are going astray, since he himself is subject to weakness. Hebrews 4:14 -5:1-2

Jesus knew we were going to have trouble. Because He knows this, He will deal gently with those who are ignorant and going astray; He will deal gently with those who are weak and are being tempted. If we are holding on to the grace of Jesus, His cross is sufficient for salvation. You just need to make sure to plant both feet firmly on the cross. Why?

Because according to the verses we already shared, some will turn away, some will say, “Lord, Lord” and He will tell them, “Get away from me, I didn’t even know you.” These are people who never really surrendered or stayed on the path. Christ’s cross will not break, but until we die, we are free to reject the work that He has done. Until we are dead, we must remain dependent upon the work of Christ. There is no other way to heaven or God.

Until we die we must follow our "in-flight" rules. If you have ever flown in a plane, you know the "Don't move around the cabin until there is no turbulence" warning is legitimate. In fact, the rougher the ride, the more comforting that seat feels. The same is true in life: The more turbulent life becomes, the more dependent we should be on the vessel of our salvation. Unfortunately, people get into the turbulence of being a Christ follower and bail out, saying, "This isn't for me." If we bail out on the cross of Christ, look at the picture and tell me what awaits us. Until death, we are free to move about on the cross going forward and backward. If we get back to the world's side, if we die still doing things our way, the only end for us is death and destruction.

Am I saying you can lose your salvation? I am saying you need to consider what Jesus said when He told us that the worries of life, the thorns of deception, the deceitfulness of wealth, and your desire to sin will cause many to turn back to what we are saved from. These are not my words; they are the words of Jesus.

If you think people were saved before they turned back, then yes, you believe they can reject Christ and walk away from what they knew to be true. If you don't think they were saved in the first place, then they can't lose it because they didn't ever have it. What I am getting at is that you must decide if you think Jesus was talking about people who had started their journey on the cross or not when He said these things. I am not going to tell you what to believe. I simply want us to understand in picture form what we are really saying when we talk about losing our salvation.

Take a look at this passage:

> *My brothers, if one of you should wander from the truth and someone should bring him back, remember this: Whoever turns a sinner from the error of his way will save him from death and cover over a multitude of sins.* James 5:19-20

Whether or not this passage in James is talking about a spiritual death or a physical death, the point of this book is to turn people to the Truth. The point of this book is to help people turn from any disobedience in their lives and surrender wholeheartedly to God so that they may become a mature Christ follower that is truly guided by the power of the Holy Spirit.

This book is not designed to define what we can get away with and still be saved. This book is designed to help people experience running to God who has amazing things in store for those who obediently surrender to him!

This book is not about sin and death, it is about life and victorious Christian living. It is not about what we are saved from, it is about what we were saved for!

I know what I believe, but I can assure you I don't have it all figured out yet. I am still being matured myself. I know what I believe, but I am in constant devotion to God, searching His Word more and more every day so I might walk a little closer to Him. I wholeheartedly believe that the conversation of eternal security could be solved with a different starting point. **Let's start asking ourselves how we can walk closer to Him, rather than how far we can live from Him and still make it to heaven.**

That is why our churches are dead. We are not teaching people where the real life is. **Real life isn't at the beginning of the journey; real life is when we live totally empowered by the Holy Spirit guiding and directing us.**

For some of us, this might take a lifetime to learn. Some of us may cross that bridge quickly and have a lifetime to bring others with us. Maybe some of us are going to spend the rest of our lives fighting this teaching.

There are other "yeah but" conversations and objections we could discuss in this chapter. I am going to end this chapter with the words Paul wrote to the Philippians:

> *But what does it matter? The important thing is that in every way, whether from false motives or true, Christ is preached. And because of this I rejoice. Yes, and I will continue to rejoice, for I know that through your prayers and the help given by the Spirit of Jesus Christ, what has happened to me will turn out for my deliverance. I eagerly expect and hope that I will in no way be ashamed, but will have sufficient courage so that now as always Christ will be exalted in my body, whether by life or by death. For to me, to live is Christ and to die is gain.* Philippians 1:18-21

Paul continues to express my deepest inclinations when he shares this statement:

> *Not that I have already obtained all this, or have already been made perfect, but I press on to take hold of that for which Christ Jesus took hold of me. Brothers, I do not consider myself yet to have taken hold of it. But one thing I do: forgetting what is*

behind and straining toward what is ahead, I press on toward the goal to win the prize for which God has called me heavenward in Christ Jesus. All of us who are mature should take such a view of things. And if on some point you think differently, that too God will make clear to you. Only let us live up to what we have already attained. Join with others in following my example, brothers, and take note of those who live according to the pattern we gave you. For, as I have often told you before and now say again even with tears, many live as enemies of the cross of Christ. Their destiny is destruction, their god is their stomach, and their glory is in their shame. Their mind is on earthly things. But our citizenship is in heaven. And we eagerly await a Savior from there, the Lord Jesus Christ, who, by the power that enables him to bring everything under his control, will transform our lowly bodies so that they will be like his glorious body. Philippians 3:12-21

There is so much more for us to do than to converse about our doctrinal differences. Let's press on to the final chapter.

LET'S GO!! – CHPT 12

It is my greatest prayer that at this point in the book you have had a stirring in your sixth sense. Maybe you have sensed that there is something missing from your walk with God, something that has been missing from your journey. If you have sensed that, then the mission of this book has been successful.

Taking it one step further, I hope to help you do something about it. There is abundant life for those who put their faith and trust in Jesus Christ.

> *The thief comes only to steal and kill and destroy; I have come that they may have life, and have it to the full. "I am the good shepherd. The good shepherd lays down his life for the sheep. I am the good shepherd; I know my sheep and my sheep know me"* John 10:10-11, 14

If you have felt a stirring in your soul, it is simply because the Holy Spirit has used this book to awaken a longing that your soul recognizes as the voice of the Shepherd. Your sixth sense is realizing that there is more for you to experience in Christ. Christ died for more than what you have realized in your journey. If you are feeling this, then I encourage you to acknowledge where you are in the pictures throughout this book.

I encourage you to acknowledge in your heart that you want to be a Hebrews Christ follower—the follower who allows the Holy Spirit to control every area of his or her life; the follower who surrenders family, future, finances, relationships, desires, and even failures to the Holy Spirit's control. **It is in total surrender that true freedom and liberty begin.** This is the key to allowing the Holy Spirit to guide your sixth sense.

You may need to do some soul searching. You may need to ask yourself if you are willing to do whatever it takes to follow the Holy Spirit. If you make this decision, you may have to experience some of the greatest pain you can imagine. When God roots out poor thinking, He goes into the inner recesses of our deepest, darkest secrets. He exposes our greatest fears and shows us the greatest giants that we will ever have to conquer. There is great deliverance and freedom for a person who is willing to take this final step, but it may be one of the most painful steps you have ever taken, depending upon your desire for control and how many poor choices you have buried. Depending on how many lies you have told others and even yourself, and how many fears and anxieties you have, this process of deliverance make take a while. When the Israelites got to enter the promised land, they had to destroy every enemy of God. The enemy was throughout the whole land. As you take this step, you must be willing to eradicate all thinking contrary to God's Word.

Remember my example of moving to North Carolina. It may seem simple to some, but the false notion that I could somehow work my way through life just believing the American dream, ran much deeper through my veins than I thought. My identity was wrapped up in my work ethic.

God had to deal with my thinking about my identity. He had to reveal some areas of weakness. My areas of weakness were not necessarily areas of what many consider sin, but my thinking had caused me to go grow dependent upon my own efforts versus God's promises. I have preached God's promises for years.

What I am desperately trying to convey is that if you genuinely want to yield every area of your life to God, be ready for Him to show you areas that you don't even think are an issue.

He sent me on a crash course of readjusted identity thinking. What he revealed to me was liberating. I didn't even know I was held captive to a poor thought process. It was like a part of my backbone that has supported me for years. I had seen God accomplish a lot with my work ethic over the years.

We have lived in North Carolina for a few years now. God guided us to an amazing church, and we have developed some amazing new friends and a great new ministry. But it came with an incredible price tag. It came with an incredible trust in God, not just from me, but my wife and my children took a huge step of faith. There are too many promises and miracles to list that have confirmed and proven God's faithful promises. And there are several unmet promises that continue to test our faith.

My guess is that you are going to have an entirely different revelation and experience along your journey, but my guess is that it will be equally painful for you and as equally fulfilling. I could have chosen to stay where I was in life. I would have continued to see God work and move in people's lives. I could have loved my family just the same in Michigan and my children would have been close to their grandma. The people I loved at my previous church wouldn't have been hurt by our leaving and many would not have gotten mad at me. My intentions and desires would not have been misunderstood, people may not have said some of the things they did.

However, if I would have stayed this book would never have been completed, and my family would never have experienced what God has done since our move. The future of what God is doing right now would have been forever altered! In twenty years, I am sure I will have an even better picture of what God is going to do with this next phase of my journey.

My deepest desire is for you to experience what He has in store for the next phase of your journey. I am here simply as an example. If you can learn from it, great. **You have been uniquely created by God to be the best you that you can be.** The best thing that you can do is embrace who God has created you to be and let Him have complete access to who you are. Trust Him at His word and watch what he can do through you.

The kingdom that God wants to establish with this sixth sense exists within your mind and your will. You cannot experience true Holy Spirit living until you surrender all, and are willing to let go of everything and never pick it back up again.

If you are ready to let go of everything and trust God entirely, then you are prepared for the next step. Get ready, because it is most likely going to be painful. If you don't like pain, then you better just stay in the wilderness. If you don't like to fight and you just want peace, then you better not try this last step because victory can only be granted once a battle has been won.

You will not be alone in your battle, although there will be times you feel like you are alone. You will not be ripped to shreds, although you will feel like you are being decimated at times. God is not mad at you, even though you may feel like it. When God corrected my thinking, he addressed a way of thought that had shaped my life for forty years. He is still showing me where it affects me. The battles are smaller now.

When God first revealed my personal giants, it literally felt like I was being given a new spine. The good news is that God is a master surgeon. It may hurt like crazy, but man up, my friend, pull up your boot straps and get ready for the God of this universe to do in you what only He can do.

If you have already experienced what I am talking about, then you are about ready to jump out of your skin. Join me as we help to raise up mature Christ followers. Let's fill our land, let's fill our churches with Holy Spirit-empowered and mature Christ followers who can properly divide the Word of Truth, who can stand up under the weight of the pressures of life, and who can lead others to the life here on earth for which Christ gave His life. Christ has so much in store for you. Will you allow the Holy Spirit complete access to your life? Don't make excuses. Don't just give lip service to the God of this universe.

I am going to give you a prayer to pray. There are no magic powers in this prayer. Put it in your own words if you want to, or repeat it verbatim. No matter what, make sure you pray it out of a sincere, pure heart. Don't pray it with reservation; don't pray it with a lack of faith, because it won't work. If you are not ready for your life to be turned upside down, don't pray it either. If you don't like internal pain, don't pray it. But if you are genuinely sick and tired of the church being powerless to change the world, and you want God to do something through you to turn as many lives back to Him as possible, then pray something like this:

Dear Holy Spirit,

I have failed many times, but you know that. I have taken you down roads that have grieved your heart, and I have been okay with it. I like to sin sometimes. I have guarded my heart from you, and I didn't even know it. I am sorry. From this point forward, I give you complete access to my sixth sense. I ask that you would guide me into all truth, first in truth to your Holy Word. I realize that the Scriptures are Your words to me; help them come alive to me. I ask that You guide me in all truth to myself. Please reveal any wrong thinking, any act of unforgiveness, any disobedience to Your word ... I give You permission to change me and reveal to me any area that I have knowingly or unknowingly kept from Your control. I ask from this point forward that You will be the one in control of all of my relationships. That You will guide me at all times in how to say what You want me to say, in how You want me to act, in how You want me to forgive or even correct. Use me from this point forward to discover what You have uniquely created me to do. Let me do it with the power that only You can provide. Holy Spirit help me to keep myself plugged into Your power source each and every day. Make my heart sensitive every day to Your leading so that my feet may not wander from the truth of Your ways. Bring me back quickly when my thoughts are not Yours. From this point forward I am Your humble and complete servant. Use me, and empower me to accomplish Your great will for my life. Thank You for hearing and answering my prayer.

Amen!

If you just prayed that prayer, and really meant it, then watch out because you are about to experience a whole new power. It could mean that your life is going to take a radical new turn in the future. It could mean that you are going to keep on doing what you are doing, but you are going to experience a whole new power. It could mean that you are about to enter the worst hell you could ever imagine, and you are going to question every moment why you would have ever prayed a prayer like that. Take it back quickly if you are not ready, because when God gets hold of stuff, He doesn't do little things. He created His church to save the world. You are His church!

Because of the magnitude of this prayer, it is imperative that you get yourself in a church that is going to help you grow and thrive. If you are in a dead church, then get out now while you can—it will only kill your spirit. The only way I don't want you to get out of a church that is dead is if God is asking you to help bring it back to life. If that is the case, my prayers just increased exponentially, because you really are about ready to experience your greatest hell. I do not mean that disrespectfully. There is no greater challenge than awakening a dead and dying church, especially if that church has money or success.

Whatever your situation in life, know this: I have prayed for you before you ever read this book. God has great things in store for you. Far greater than my prayers are the prayers that Christ gives for us all the time as our great High Priest. Far greater than my prayers are the prayers that the Holy Spirit is praying for you, even at this very moment.

I look forward to hearing about what God does as a result of you living as a Hebrews Christian, totally surrendered to the Holy Spirit as He guides your sixth sense into all truth.

Be blessed brothers and sisters as we join together to change the world for the Gospel of Jesus Christ.

ABOUT THE AUTHOR

Don Gentry lives in Charlotte NC with his incredible wife and three wonderful daughters. Don and Stacy have been married since 1997 and have experienced God in their life and marriage in amazing ways.

Don has served in ministry for over 26 years. He has served as a youth pastor, senior pastor, family pastor, and executive pastor. He currently serves as the Executive Pastor of Journey Church in Huntersville NC.

It is his greatest passion in life to help others experience a personal and passionate relationship with the creator of this universe by bringing simplicity and understanding to how God relates to humans through the work of the Holy Spirit.

Made in the USA
Columbia, SC
15 July 2018